Pathways

TONY EVANS

Pathways

From Providence to Purpose

B&H
PUBLISHING GROUP
NASHVILLE, TENNESSEE

978-1-4336-8660-3

Published by B&H Publishing Group
Nashville, Tennessee

Dewey Decimal Classification: 231.5
Subject Heading: PROVIDENCE AND GOVERNMENT OF
GOD / CHRISTIAN LIFE / ESTHER, QUEEN

Chapter One Note: portions are lifted from *The Kingdom Agenda*,
Moody Publishers, 1,000 words.

Cover design by Faceout Studio. Imagery © istock/releon8211,
shutterstock/Emre Tarimcioglu, and shutterstock/rustamank.
Author photo © Joshua Farris.

1 2 3 4 5 6 • 22 21 20 19

ACKNOWLEDGMENTS

I want to thank my friends at B&H Publishing, particularly Jennifer Lyell, Devin Maddox, and Taylor Combs for their work in seeing this project come to life on these pages. My appreciation also goes out to Heather Hair, on this monumental fiftieth book and/or Bible study we have completed together, for her skills and insights in collaboration on this manuscript.

CONTENTS

Setting the Stage

 Everybody loves a story.

A good story. A grand story. A spectacular story.

A story of mystery, intrigue, suspense, and surprise with, of course, some sparkle spread within.

Such is the story of Esther.

Such is the story of Gideon.

Such is the story of Cinderella.

Such is the story of Pederson.

Now, stick with me—even if you've never heard of the name Pederson. I realize this name may have thrown you a bit. And while you might not recognize who he is, I would wager that you will recognize what he did.

But let's start with someone else first. Let's start with someone we all know.

Cue Cinderella.

Cinderella is a fictional character who somehow comes across as more real than many people we know. Maybe it's because we can identify with the hope of her story. We long for her trajectory to be our own. Cinderella started out living with a wicked stepmother and two equally wicked stepsisters. Essentially, she was made to live as a slave. The problem with Cinderella was that she got stuck there. She became locked in a situation which she had no control to change.

But you know how the story turns, twists, and flips for the characters involved. You know about the ball, and that through a series of miraculous interventions, she was transported to the ball in a carriage. There she met a prince. The prince saw Cinderella and loved her. But the problem in the story, as you know, is that the clock struck midnight. When the clock hit midnight, she reverted back to her old place. She became a slave again to an evil step-mother and two evil stepsisters.

The amazing part of Cinderella's story is that the prince never forgot her. Even though there had been a lot of people at the ball, there was something about her that made her stand out from the crowd. She was special. She was unique. She was rare. Everyone wanted the prince, but the prince wanted Cinderella.

All he had to work with in order to find her again, though, was a shoe that she had left behind. If he could find the foot that fit the shoe, he would have found Cinderella. So he set out going house to house in search of his princess. After a long and hard search, the prince finally found Cinderella. And, as the story goes, they lived happily ever after.

Hers is a rags-to-riches story whose familiarity is nearly equal to us all. Hers is a great story, which lights up the eyes of hearers from toddlers to adults. But her story is fiction. It's not true. The one I'm about to tell you is as true as they come. It's not about a prince or a princess. But it does end with a trip to a castle, if that helps. It's about Pederson, a man most of you may not know at all.

Even if you are one of those few who doesn't follow football or fancy sports, most people do know who wins the annual showdown known as the Super Bowl. Nearly half of all Americans tune in, according to Nielson. Headlines dominate friends' social media posts and the actual news alike for weeks on end. It's hard to miss who grabbed that shiny silver trophy at the end of each season. Especially when it is an upset. Especially when it is an unexpected win. Especially when an underdog comes out on top, or perhaps (in the case of Doug Pederson) we can call them an "underbird."

Pederson did coach the *Eagles,* after all. And the Eagles did pull off one of the most unexpected victories of all time in the 2017–2018 NFL season. In fact, they did it more than once; they did it thrice. Yes, three times.

The Eagles were officially the underdogs going into each of their three post-season playoff games. No one thought they could win. Each and every week, no one believed they could beat the team that had been pitted against them. No one gave them any chance at all. Except for them, that is.

But I'm getting ahead of myself.

Why did no one give this team a chance, despite a winning record on the season and home-field advantage in two of the three games? Well, in football, you need to know that the quarterback is king. In fact, many consider him to be the most critical player on the field. That's why quarterbacks get paid the largest salaries. They can carry a team on their shoulders or toss them away for a loss simply based on how they play. Lose your star quarterback and you may just lose the entire season.

Take a look at the Green Bay Packers in the same season, as an example. Heading into week six of the NFL season, they had four wins to just one loss under the prowess of their quarterback Aaron Rodgers. Yet after Rodgers broke his collarbone in that game, the team tallied up only three wins to a whopping eight losses in the remainder of the season. Lose the king and you lose the chance at getting the victory crown.

Or so they say.

Which is exactly what they did say about Pederson's Eagles when their star quarterback, Carson Wentz, went down and out with a season-ending injury and still two games left in the year. While the Eagles had been on the pathway to the playoffs up until that time, nearly everyone—including myself—wrote them off after that. After all, how could any team make it to the Super Bowl on the arm of a backup quarterback?

Not only that, but Coach Pederson had only been a head coach in the NFL for two years. In fact, a decade earlier he was coaching a Christian high school team. Yes, *high school*. And a decade before coaching high school? Well, Pederson was just a backup quarterback in the same city (Philadelphia) for the same team (Eagles) he now coached in the playoffs. And sure, while most people might assume that's actually a good thing, it wasn't in Pederson's case.

This is because fans in Philadelphia hated him. They didn't want him on their team. In fact, fans hated Pederson so much that they would literally spit on him when he walked out of the tunnel and onto the field. Now, if you think getting spit on is bad, it only got worse as the games wore on. Eventually, the fans expressed their hatred for Pederson by throwing batteries at him, along with their beer.[1] Now, whether you follow football or not, you can probably discern that for a fan to throw the over-priced beer which is sold at the game just so he can express his emotions . . . well, that's saying a lot. They hated him.

These were fans from Philadelphia too. These were not the attendees from other cities. These were Eagles fans throwing batteries and beer at their own backup quarterback Doug Pederson. That's how much they did not want him on their team. That's how much they did not want him to play. And, well, that's not normal. It's not normal for fans to do that to one of their own players. Especially in a city whose very name—Philadelphia—means "brotherly love." This hatred ran deep. And while I can imagine those batteries hit hard, I bet the humiliation hurt even more.

"It was those large ones . . . those 'D' ones," Pederson would later say when asked to recount his previous stint in Philadelphia shortly after being hired to coach the team. Not such fond memories from a city with not-much-brotherly-love after all.

But despite the beer and despite the batteries ("those large ones . . . those 'D' ones") thrown at him decades earlier, Pederson had made the choice to come back to Philadelphia to coach. He had come back to coach in a city that once loathed him.

And here they were now entering the playoffs with Pederson at the helm. Pederson would need courage, wisdom, restraint, and faith to lead this underdog along the pathway to victory. This was the team, after all, whom everyone had written off when they had lost their starting quarterback weeks earlier. This was also the team whose highest-paid player was on the defensive side of the ball. (That's inside talk for no huge stars at all.) Without an offense to score points, football games are rarely won. Let alone playoff games against the best of the best. And certainly not a Super Bowl against the dynasty known and feared as the 5-time champions, the New England Patriots, whose quarterback Tom Brady goes by the name "Comeback King." This wasn't just a David and Goliath battle. This was David and a whole army of Goliaths.

But this also wasn't the first time Coach Pederson had found himself on the path of what most considered to be a no-win competition. Remember when I mentioned he coached high school football years before? That history is important because it was in the context of his past that Pederson learned what he needed for his present. God's providential placement had Pederson in the trenches of a similar battle years before he would come onto the national, and international, stage. It was there that he was sharpened, humbled, encouraged, led, and developed. It was there that his team, Calvary Baptist, faced their own Goliath of sorts. And it was there that Pederson learned how to lead an underdog to victory.

The opponent was known as Evangel. And despite Evangel's seventeen-year undefeated streak against district opponents, Pederson prepared his team to face them with confidence. Despite Evangel's decisive previous wins over Calvary Baptist with scores resembling credit card security codes more than football scores (55–3 and 42–6), he motivated his players to believe they could win. And despite Evangel being a nationally ranked team with nine players on the offense being named D-1 (a high honor in high school football), somehow and someway Pederson managed to put together a team to win when winning meant the most.

It might have been the hours upon hours he required his players to spend with him watching game film before school, during lunch, and after school again. Many players later recalled how they studied more film in high school than they were ever asked to study at college or in the NFL.

It also might have been the one-on-one comradery Pederson instilled in his players by getting on their level and practicing with them while holding nothing back from his own 6 feet 3, 230 pounds strength. Even to the point that he literally broke several of his players' fingers with the power of his passes.

It could be that Pederson raised their level of confidence by speaking to them in ways reflective of how he felt about them and not according to what others said. He calibrated their own convictions about their skills based on what he believed and not on what the culture said concerning their capacity, or lack thereof. On a level of football where one- or two-word plays was considered the standard for what players could handle, Pederson raised that standard and gave his players much more complicated plays. For example, instead of "Spread Right" being called on its own, he had them remember things like, "Spread Right 76 Smash Minus Over Protection," and then some.

This alone demonstrated how much Pederson believed in them. And, as a result, Pederson's players wound up believing in themselves too.

Calvary Baptist went on to beat their Goliath, toppling that seventeen-year district win streak. A decade later, Pederson's Eagles went on to beat their Goliath too, cutting off the head of the most dominant dynasty in this decade of football.

What's more is that the Eagles did it with that backup quarterback few people believed could, Nick Foles. This is the same backup quarterback who had doubts about himself as well, when he contemplated retiring from football altogether just a year before this game. This is also the same backup quarterback whose childhood hero played opposite him in this final Bird vs. Goliath Super Bowl. The same backup quarterback who had been cut from another team just two seasons before, with his release from that team embarrassingly captured on television for the whole world to see. The coach who had let him go casually dismissed him by saying, "Hey—good luck. And I hope you land on your feet."

Yes, that backup quarterback. He did more than land on his feet, though. He flew.

This same backup quarterback flew through Super Bowl LII, throwing for nearly four hundred yards and three touchdowns. Not only that, but he also set a record with the opposing team's quarterback, his childhood hero, for most offensive yards in the history of all Super Bowls. Oh, and yes, he did something more. He set his own record as well, becoming the first quarterback to ever catch a touchdown in a Super Bowl. You read that right—*catch*.

In a bizarre twist of fate, the guy on the team who throws the ball actually caught it for a touchdown. This remarkable play, something that had never happened before, is now known forever by fans worldwide as the "Philly Special."

The Philly Special

It was fourth and goal from the one-yard line in the second quarter of the game. That early on in a game, most coaches would settle for kicking a field goal. Especially a coach with a backup quarterback on hand. But not Pederson. He believed in Foles. He believed in his athletic abilities. The same coach who had taught his high schoolers eight-word plays wound up boiling this next play down to just two. It was called the *Philly Special*. And, oh, was it special. So special that the team sought to keep it quiet in the weeks leading up to the game by rarely even practicing it during the regular workouts. It was later reported that they had practiced the "play" in the Radisson Hotel in the Mall of America to try and keep the surprise factor in place for the opponent. I can tell you that the rest of us watching were just as surprised as the Eagles hoped.

Fourth and goal is often a run-play if a play is to be run at all. But instead, Pederson and Foles talked before the call and Foles urged him to run the *Special*,[2] a gutsy call to say the least. To throw to your backup quarterback on fourth down when you are playing against Goliath and the Comeback King where every single point matters is not something anyone else would probably ever do.

But Pederson called the play. Foles relayed it to his teammates in the huddle, eyes widening as they heard. Then the center hiked the ball to the running back who then gave it to the tight end who then threw it to the quarterback who then hauled it in for the score.

Touchdown Eagles!

Fans went wild. Announcers hit replay again and again and again. It's as if they couldn't believe it unless they saw it for the third, fourth, fifth, or sixth time. The stadium shook as it would at a Gladiator event. Undecided fans started rooting for Philadelphia. After all, who doesn't love a Cinderella story? Which is exactly what Foles, Pederson, and the rest of the Eagles lived out right before millions of our eyes. Later named the Super Bowl MVP, Foles even went to Cinderella's castle with his wife and daughter for the obligatory Disney World parade the very next day.

But maybe football isn't quite biblical enough for you or for setting up the subject we are about to journey into together on God's providential hand. Perhaps a Cinderella story shouldn't be where I start to set the stage. Would it help if I went straight to Scripture itself and we looked at a man named Gideon?

Or maybe I don't even need to do that myself. Another Eagles player already did. In a postgame interview on how the Eagles pulled off this victory, the tight end who made the magical pass, Trey Burton, said,

> Our team? The only thing I can really compare it to is the story of Gideon. There is a story of Gideon in Judges 7 in the Bible where a bunch of people go into a battle and God tells them it's too much—too many guys, and if they go to battle with that many people, God wouldn't get the glory.

Burton then encouraged the sports reporter to go read the story of Gideon for himself, finishing up with, "It's really similar to what happened to the guys with this team."[3]

Likewise, the former star quarterback who had to sit the Super Bowl out due to an injury said something like this in a social media post. He had put it up the morning of the big game. Wentz posted a photo of himself sitting next to Foles, along with this:

> God's writing an unbelievable story, and he's getting all the glory! Let's roll boys. #FlyEaglesFly[4]

God's writing an unbelievable story. Which is exactly what God loves to do. Time and time again, He maneuvers, moves, tweaks, twists, turns, and flips the script of life in order to pen a story for the ages. He wrote one for the Eagles. He wrote one for Gideon. He wrote one for Pederson. He wrote one for Esther. He is writing one for you.

God writes the kinds of stories where what you wind up reading isn't what you expected to read at all. These are storybook endings to improbable, even impossible, situations.

But the key to arriving at your own storybook ending in life is what we will explore in these pages together. The key to your arrival comes in how you handle the path. It comes in whether or not you even remain on the path, as well as in how you respond when situations turn south real fast. Do you hesitate? Do you quit? Do you choose an easier, better lit path instead?

> *God's writing an unbelievable story. Which is exactly what God loves to do.*

The key to your arrival at the destined purpose God has for you comes in how you navigate around the thrown beer and D-sized batteries that life has a way of throwing at you.

Who do you listen to when others say that you will never live up to your own dreams and desires?

Whose voice guides you when people say you'll never make anything of yourself?

Or when it appears that the relationship you are struggling to keep will never be restored?

The career could never take off. The finances could never be reversed. They give up on you, with an obligatory sentiment of sympathy, "I hope you land on your feet."

But like Cinderella, like Foles, like Pederson, like Gideon, and like Esther, the key to reaching your destiny is staying on the providential pathway God has set you on, despite your desire to quit. It's learning how to fly despite your inability to even, at times, walk. It's discovering the power of perspective and the fuel of faith.

It's in understanding and embracing the doctrine of providence, even when it looks like God is nowhere to be found.

No other story in the Bible highlights this doctrine for us as clearly as the story of Esther. The story of Esther is a shocker because what you read in chapter after chapter and verse after verse is not what is supposed to happen. There are lives toppled who had once looked secure. There are twists and turns that come unexpected.

But there is something else about the story of Esther that sets it apart from all other stories in the Bible. This book is unique among the sixty-six books that comprise the Canon because it never mentions God's name. It is the only book with no direct reference to God. Every other book mentions God over and over and over again. But in the ten chapters of Esther, you will not find the name of God at all. Which creates a question: Why would God put in His canonical writings something that never mentions Him?

I believe it is because God wanted to use this Cinderella story to teach us something about Him. He wanted to help us see His fingerprints. To teach us how to identify them. To reveal to us what it looks like when He organizes and maneuvers things toward His providential plan. God will often stay in the background while controlling the activity of the foreground. We may not overtly see Him in the various situations of our lives, but He is the great Puppet-Master, pulling the strings by either causing or allowing things to happen toward His intended end.

He makes this point crystal clear to us in this Cinderella story of sorts. He gives us a peek behind the curtain, equipping us with the tools we need to discern when He is working and how best to follow His lead. And He does it all through a story. It's true that our minds and hearts love the art of a good story, thus Esther has been scripted in story form. It's a motion picture, if you will, displayed on the screens of our souls.

Thus, unlike most books I write and sermons I preach which revolve around a topic or principle, this one will follow the pathway of the narrative from start to finish. We'll go through each chapter of Esther's book as if we were watching it play out on the screen or on a stage. We will progress as it progresses. Walk where it takes us. Turn where it turns. Climb, or descend, as the story does. In so doing, we will gain insights as the insights are revealed, as each chapter unfolds before us.

My hope for this book is that in reading it, you will learn to discover the power of providence in the midst of your personal pain, fear, gain, loss, and even love. What's more, I want you to discover the very personal nature of God as He maneuvers humanity along multiple pathways, intersecting each of us in His intended aim. God is the greatest storyteller—the Puppet-Master behind the scenes. When you learn how to locate Him in the midst of what appears to be His absence, trusting Him along the dark pathways life often offers, you will be perfectly positioned on your own unique pathway of purpose. It is on that path where you will discover in what ways you, too, have been created and placed in your own spectacular story for such a time as this.

CHAPTER ONE

The Puppet-Master

Read the prologue.

Many people skip it—in fact, most people skip it. But I highly recommend you go back and read the prologue if you did skip it. It sets the stage for the story. It lays the stones toward the pathway we are about to trod on together. It gives the context for why we are here. It introduces us to the Puppet-Master.

God is the great Puppet-Master, working behind the curtains of what we can see. With a slight twitch of His hand, He can change an entire scene. With the movement of His arm, He rearranges the characters in the narrative of your day. God is constantly moving, turning, maneuvering, and establishing all things in His providence toward His intended aim. Even, and especially, when you cannot see Him at all.

No metaphor is perfect, so it's important, before we move forward, to point out one caveat. Puppets do not have freedom. They are unable to make choices. The amazing thing about God's providence is that He is able to work all things according to His purposes *without negating human freedom and choices.* Though we cannot fully understand how this is possible, the Bible is clear on these two truths: God is sovereign, and humans really and truly choose their actions.

There are many times in life's circumstances when you look for God and He is simply un-locatable. We all know this. We all experience this. There are many times when it seems like God is allowing things to happen to you that, if He truly cared about you, He would never allow them to happen at all. Kind of like Pederson getting the D-sized batteries and beer thrown at his head. (*It's in the prologue.*)

Then there are those times when your needs mount, your confusion culminates in chaos, and you wonder which way to go. Yet it seems like God is not there to guide you. It feels as if you are walking along a dark, scary path alone.

Like the biblical character Job, you may scratch your head and whisper quietly enough so that no one around you hears your fear. Like Job, you may wonder where God even is. Like Job, you may mumble quietly, "But if I go to the east, he is not there; if I go to the west, I do not find him. When he is at work in the north, I do not see him; when he turns to the south, I catch no glimpse of him" (Job 23:8–9 NIV).

Job felt alone. Job felt forgotten. Job felt forsaken by God Himself.

Have you ever felt like Job? If we were to be honest, we all have. It's human to feel this way. God's seen it before. He knows our frame. He knows we are just modified dust (Ps. 103:14). It is in those times when we just want God to show up with some skin on so He can let us know He is still there. It is in those times when we reach for Him, but like the wind, He escapes our grasp. It is in those times when His invisible hand eludes us even while His words continue to urge us to keep walking the path He has called us on. But do we take the next step? Do we walk in faith? Or do we refuse to move forward, wanting instead to hear our own version of the whispered words we've read on the dusty pages of Scripture where God lets it be known He is there? Words such as:

> "Do not fear, for I have redeemed you; I have called you by your name; you are mine. I will be with you when you pass through the waters, and when you pass through the rivers, they will not overwhelm you. You will not be scorched when you walk through the fire, and the flame will not burn you. For I am the LORD your God, the Holy One of Israel, and your Savior." (Isa. 43:1b–3a)

> "I will be the same until your old age, and I will bear you up when you turn gray. I have made you, and I will carry you; I will bear and rescue you." (Isa. 46:4)

"I will go before you and level the uneven places; I will shatter the bronze doors and cut the iron bars in two. I will give you the treasures of darkness and riches from secret places, so that you may know that I am the LORD. I am the God of Israel, who calls you by your name." (Isa. 45:2–3)

"Be strong and courageous; don't be terrified or afraid of them. For the LORD your God is the one who will go with you; he will not leave you or abandon you." (Deut. 31:6)

"Haven't I commanded you: be strong and courageous? Do not be afraid or discouraged, for the LORD your God is with you wherever you go." (Josh. 1:9)

We long to hear something like that. Anything, really. Assurances from God to let us know that He knows where we are and where He is taking us. Assurances that we should not be afraid, but rather have courage and rest in His presence and power. Even when it seems as if He is nowhere to be found.

If you have ever felt like that, my friend, you are not alone. In fact, it is such a common occurrence that God speaks a lot about it in His Word. There is even a theology tied to His invisibility. It is a theology known as *providence*.

The providence of God—a doctrinal subset underneath the overarching doctrine known as *sovereignty*—is such a critical spiritual truth that knowing and living by it can radically transform your life. When you are able to discern how God providentially works in history as well as in the present, you are able to move along the pathways of life with a purpose and intention that will propel you forward. Even in those moments, days, weeks, months, or even years when you don't seem to see God, feel God, or hear from God at all, you will know that He is pulling the strings behind the scenes. He is the Great Puppet-Master, directing your divine destiny on this stage called life. Knowing this will enable you to make choices according to His will and kingdom agenda, rather than out of your own reaction for self-preservation or control.

In fact, one of God's chief theological attributes is His sovereignty. Sovereignty simply refers to His rulership over all of His creation. According to Ephesians 1:11, He does all things after the counsel of His own will. In Romans 11:36 we read, "For from him and through him and to him are all things."

Absolutely nothing escapes His rule and influence. God is in charge of all things because He has created and sustains all things.

Thus, as we start our journey together through the depths, clefts, and mountaintops that make up God's providential terrain, understanding His kingdom gives us the markers which guide our travel. But to understand God's rule, we must first understand what He rules: His kingdom.

> *Absolutely nothing escapes His rule and influence.*

Now, if you are an American, you are most likely an American because you were born here. If you are a part of the kingdom of

God, it is because you have been born again into His kingdom. The reason why you do not want to miss a full comprehension of the kingdom as you seek to understand providence and sovereignty is not only because it affects your understanding of these two things, but it also is the key to understanding the entire Bible. The unifying central theme throughout the Bible is the glory of God and the advancement of His kingdom. The conjoining thread from Genesis to Revelation—from beginning to end—is focused on one thing: God's glory through advancing God's kingdom.

When you do not understand that theme, then the Bible becomes disconnected stories that are great for inspiration but seem to be unrelated in purpose and direction. The Bible exists to share God's movement in history toward the establishment and expansion of His kingdom, highlighting the connectivity throughout which is the kingdom. Understanding that increases the relevancy of this several-thousand-year-old manuscript to your day-to-day living, because the kingdom is not only then, it is now.

Throughout the Bible, the kingdom of God is His rule, His plan, His program. God's kingdom is all-embracing. It covers everything in the universe. In fact, we can define the kingdom as God's comprehensive rule over all creation. It is the rule of God and not the rule of man that is paramount.

Now if God's kingdom is comprehensive, so is His kingdom agenda. The kingdom agenda, then, may be defined as *the visible manifestation of the comprehensive rule of God over every area of life*. That has serious implications for us. The reason so many of us believers are struggling is that we want God to bless our agenda rather than us fulfilling His. We want God to okay our plans rather than our fulfilling His. We want God to bring us glory rather than us bringing glory to Him.

But it doesn't work that way. God has only one plan—His kingdom plan. We need to find out what that is so we can make sure we're working on God's plan, not ours.

The Greek word the Bible uses for kingdom is *basileia*, which basically means a "rule" or "authority." Included in this definition is the concept of power. So when we talk about a kingdom, we're talking first about a king or a ruler. We're talking about someone who is in charge. Now if there is a ruler, there also have to be "rulees," or kingdom subjects. In addition, a kingdom includes a realm; that is, a domain over which the king rules. If you're going to have a ruler, rulees, and a realm, you also need kingdom regulations, guidelines that govern the relationship between the ruler and the subjects. These are necessary so that the rulees will know whether they are doing what the ruler wants done. Finally, there are also rebels. All of us begin rebelling against the rule of God; it takes His softening work in our hearts to turn us from rebels into rulees.

God's kingdom includes all of these elements. He is the absolute ruler of His domain, which encompasses all of creation. Likewise, His authority is total. Everything God rules, He runs—even when it doesn't look like He's running it. Even when life looks like it's out of control, God is running its "out-of-controlness."

God's kingdom also has its "rules." Colossians 1:13 says that everybody who has trusted the Lord Jesus Christ as Savior has been transferred from the kingdom of darkness to the kingdom of light. If you are a believer in Jesus Christ, your allegiance has been changed. You no longer align yourself with Satan but with Christ.

And just in case there's any doubt, let me say right now that there are no in-between kingdoms, no shades of gray here. There are only two realms in creation: the kingdom of God and the kingdom of Satan. We are subjects of one or the other.

The problem we have in the Christian culture today is that people misdefine God's kingdom. Some people secularize and politicize the kingdom, which means they think the solutions to our problems are going to fly into town on *Air Force One*. God's kingdom agenda is much bigger than the political and social realm; neither is it limited to the walls of the church. When you were saved, the kingdom of God was set up within you so that it might be best positioned to reach outwardly while directing the circumference of your life.

Getting into God's kingdom is through conversion, but getting God's kingdom into the manifestations of your everyday life comes through commitment and discipleship.

Trusting Jesus Christ for your salvation will get you to heaven. But trusting Jesus Christ for your salvation doesn't automatically get heaven to come down to you.

Getting into God's kingdom is through conversion, but getting God's kingdom into the manifestations of your everyday life comes through commitment and discipleship.

Commitment results only when the Jesus you placed your faith in is also the Jesus who rules within you—in the kingdom of which you are a part. God's kingdom goal is to manifest in history the operations of heaven in every area of your life. Therefore, when history is not reflecting heaven (Your will be done on earth as it is in heaven" [Matt. 6:10]), then God's kingdom is not visible. His kingdom is only visible when history emulates heaven. His providence is only palatable when the byways and pathways of His kingdom are the ones you choose to travel.

Linking Sovereignty and Providence

Providence references how God controls the spinning wheel of history behind the scenes. As I mentioned earlier, it is a subset of sovereignty. In other words, one way that He achieves His sovereignty is by His providence. The providence of God is the miraculous and mysterious way in which He intersects and interconnects things in order to bring about His sovereignty.

God's sovereignty is what He wants to happen.

God's providence is where He sets things up and connects them so that His sovereignty does happen.

Where we often misunderstand things is in the area of providence. This is because without a full awareness of where things are headed (sovereignty), we might wonder about the providential choices of God along the way. There are times when God will allow or even cause things to happen that seemingly appear to be in contradiction to what He wants. For God to achieve His ultimate sovereign purposes, He will at times providentially allow things to take place that are outside of His preferences. This is because in His sovereignty, God will allow things He does not prefer in order to accomplish His ultimate plan. It is only when you understand the link between providence and sovereignty that you will become conscious of God's fingerprints in the midst of His "apparent" absence. He will often only leave behind fingerprints that show up when dusted. We don't always get to see how God weaves and twists and tweaks things to take us to our intended destination and purpose. He operates behind the scenes, pulling the strings and setting the stage in ways that sometimes confuse, frustrate, and confound us. But also in ways that produce the greatest outcome and result.

Take baking a cake, for example. If you were to consider eating butter, eggs, flour, sugar, or any other ingredient in a cake all by itself, you would wind up with a mess that tastes awful. No one puts a tablespoon of flour straight into their mouth. You just don't do that. What you do, instead, is blend them together in order to create a cake. Something delightful results out of the combination, not out of each thing examined and eaten on its own.

Similarly, your destiny results out of the combination of providential ingredients mixed together and often, like a cake baked in an oven, is sealed through the heat and fire of testing, trials, and challenges. When you and I look at our individual situations on their own, it's often easy to feel overwhelmed or less-than-satisfied. That's why wrapping your mind around the link between providence and sovereignty is essential in motivating your participation on this path. Otherwise, you may just want to give up instead.

Friend, God can take the flour of your failures, the sugar of your successes, the cream of your circumstances, and mix them all together in His sovereign blender to achieve His purposes through His providence. And to illustrate how this works, He placed a book called Esther within the Canon of Scripture so that we would see an entire story where His name does not even appear, and no overt references of Him are made. He did this to support His truth which says:

> Truly you are a God who has been hiding himself, the God and Savior of Israel. (Isa. 45:15 NIV)

> A person's heart plans his way, but the LORD determines his steps. (Prov. 16:9)

> Many plans are in a person's heart, but the LORD's decree will prevail. (Prov. 19:21)

> No wisdom, no understanding, and no counsel will prevail against the LORD. (Prov. 21:30)

The Lᴏʀᴅ foils the plans of the nations; he thwarts the purposes of the peoples. But the plans of the Lᴏʀᴅ stand firm forever, the purposes of his heart through all generations. (Ps. 33:10–11 ɴɪᴠ)

God *is* sovereign, yes. But because He has granted freedom to us as human beings, He has to incorporate providential involvement in order to achieve His sovereignty. He will not allow our freedom to thwart His purposes, so He must stitch the freedom of humanity into His plans in such a way as to create a tapestry called destiny. This includes even using (never condoning) sin, sinners, and Satan to accomplish His sovereign purposes.

Before we dive into the story of Esther, let's take a deeper look at these principles of sovereignty to set the stage for the saga we'll explore. Consider it the cake platter upon which the cake will one day sit. Our understanding of sovereignty is the foundation for all else to come.

God's Overarching Goal

One of the most referenced Scriptures when it comes to this truth is Romans 8:28. You may even know it by heart. It's a favorite verse of many people. It is a powerful verse because it brings to light this issue of sovereignty and also of providence. It says, "And we know that God causes all things to work together for good to those who love God, to those who are called according to His purpose" (ɴᴀsʙ).

The key word in this passage is *causes*. God's position as supreme ruler over all that He has created gives Him the opportunity and responsibility to "cause" whatever He wants to cause. No matter how difficult the journey, no matter how challenging the trip, and no matter how precarious the pathways, providence means God caused it for a greater purpose.

Most of you have probably heard of the city Providence, Rhode Island. This city was named Providence as the colonies were being established. The pilgrims felt that God had overseen the events leading them to their safe arrival as well as the provisions that were made for them when they landed. Thus, they attached God's sovereign intervention to the name of where they chose to reside. It would serve as a constant reminder that despite how things may have once appeared, He had a destination He had been taking them to all along.

Providence is God's governance of all events, which means by exclusion that there is really no such thing as luck, chance, or happenstance. There is nothing left to fate at all. Romans 8:28 doesn't say that God causes some things to work together. Rather, it says He causes them *all*.

> *There is really no such thing as luck, chance, or happenstance.*

And while the pilgrims may have named their town of Providence rightly, not all of our founding fathers had an accurate understanding of God's invisible hand. A good number of them were what is called "deists." Deists are those who believe in a God who created everything but then left it alone to run itself. This is sort of like winding up a clock and then letting that wind work its way out on its own. In a sense, a deist believes that God has abandoned His creation to churn its way through the natural laws He established. Thus, God is a long-distance God to them. He is not eminently involved in day-to-day life.

Yet the principle of providence argues that God has not abandoned the world, but rather works within His creation to *cause* everything to conform to His unchangeable will. In fact, Colossians 1:17 says clearly, "He is before all things, and by him all things hold together." Not only does He hold everything together, He holds us together too. Acts 17 records:

> The God who made the world and everything in it—he is Lord of heaven and earth—does not live in shrines made by hands. Neither is he served by human hands, as though he needed anything, since he himself gives *everyone* life and breath and all things. (vv. 24–25, emphasis added)

Everything you and I have has been given to us as a direct result of God choosing to do so. There is nothing that you have received that was not either created by God or created by things that God created. You might want to read that sentence again, or underline it. It's important. God produces each and every single thing. Because He does, He claims sovereignty over it all as well. He controls it. He is the consummate, and ultimate, micromanager. He is intricately, intimately involved in every single detail. He manages the universe and all of us in it to the highest degree possible. And if He didn't—if He just took a moment to step back and not hold the universe in place—we would all be obliterated in an instant.

From His vantage point, it all makes perfect sense. Yet from ours, time can seem marked by an endless array or series of contingencies that we may call "luck" or "chance" or even "random events."

But that's just how it seems; that's not how it is. Because nothing is random with God. He is working out the details of everything, not just watching it transpire. What's more is that He is working out the details toward His intended goal. Once you and I come to understand His overarching goal, we can begin to understand His pathways.

God's ultimate goal always results in God's glory. Ephesians chapter 1 highlights this for us:

> In love He predestined us to adoption as sons through Jesus Christ to Himself, according to the kind intention of His will, to the praise of the glory of His grace . . . to the end that we who were the first to hope in Christ would be to the praise of His glory . . . with a view to the redemption of God's own possession, to the praise of His glory. (vv. 4b–6a, 12, 14b NASB)

The primary reason God is working everything out toward His intended outcome is "to the praise of His glory." God sets about to guarantee all that He has created fulfills and satisfies its created purpose, which is to bring glory back to Himself.

Like it or not, God exists for His own glory. Now, you can fight that truth, fuss at it, argue it, not want it, reject it, accuse it, or anything else you want to do. But whatever you do about it, it's not going to change it. God exists for God. So does everything He made. He made it for Him. That's the reason it's here. That's the reason we're here. We are made for God. Our lives are not about us; they are about Him and His glory. If you don't care for that too much, then go and make your own universe, because He made this one, so He gets to set the rules.

> *The primary reason God is working everything out toward His intended outcome is "to the praise of His glory."*

Anything that competes with, negates, or downplays God's glory exists in a perpetual state of misalignment. It is out of order. God made *all* things to display His attributes, character, and power.

There is another reason, though, why God causes all things to work together. He does it for His glory, yes, but He also does it for us—for good. You'll recall Romans 8:28 says, ". . . causes all things to work together for good . . ." (NASB). Essentially, that means He is bringing about our benefit. The word *good* means "that which is beneficial." Thus, God is also seeking to bring about benefits and blessings in our own lives as well, in the lives of those who love Him and walk according to the paths of His purpose.

Please don't misread that verse to make it apply to everyone, everywhere. Too many people do that. It does not say that God causes all things in every single way to work out for good. No, it specifically refers to those who love Him and are called according to His purpose. Thus, there is bad in this world. Negative things do happen. The assumption that is often made when they do is that God must not be good Himself. But the presence of darkness doesn't negate the power of light. Light exists to drive out darkness, not to eliminate it entirely. Romans 8:28 doesn't say that God causes all things to *be* good. Rather, He integrates all things to work together *for* good in the lives of those who love Him and follow His paths. His is the invisible hand operating behind the scenes of the good, bad, and ugly in life. He manipulates and maneuvers the many circumstances toward His intended end.

One of our difficulties in remaining on the right path as we head toward our purpose is that we do not see the end. We get frustrated and feel lost when we can't see where we are headed. Have you ever felt frustrated when you were driving and you got lost? Or have you been with someone who got frustrated when they were driving and got lost? Yet when a map was found, or a GPS, or directions from a stranger that pointed the way—the frustrations fell away. This is because reaching the end came into sight.

What happens to us, though, in following God along the pathways of His providential leading is that He doesn't always give us the directions to the very end. He doesn't provide us with the full map view so we can see every turn we'll eventually take. He gives us a glimpse here, or a direction there, but rarely ever the entire picture. Thus, people often live in a perpetual state of frustration not knowing how each step, each day, each set of circumstances or conversations are leading to the right place. Without a full view of providence tied to a surrender to sovereignty, these frustrations can mount into an overwhelming cascade of emotions threatening you like an avalanche on a blizzardy day.

Friend, nothing comes to you that doesn't pass through God's providential fingers first. You have to know that. You have to believe that. You have to trust that. You have to rest in that. That mind-set will situate you so that you can respond to life's challenges, setbacks, and apparent randomness with a spirit of intentionality and persevering faith.

When you recognize the idiosyncratic elements of the invisible hand of God, you will discover the details and direction leading you to your destiny.

CHAPTER TWO

Seeing the Invisible Hand

People rarely like providence.

It's true. Only when that providence is ushering us toward a seen result with visible rewards do we embrace providence. Why? Because we, as people, prefer autonomy. Providence precludes itself to God's rule. When we understand and accept God's providence, we are laying down our own paths, our own pursuits, and our own maneuverings to try and get us where we feel we need to go. We are letting go. We don't like to let go. But providence lifts our hand. Providence acknowledges that ultimately God *is* in control, and that His method of being in control often involves twists, turns, and meanderings which cause us concern.

Yet the sovereign providence of God can only mean that He is the absolute ruler, controller, and sustainer of all aspects of His creation. He is the sovereign King. He is running the universe. He is, to piggyback off of a popular musical, the "greatest showman" of all time. His prowess and wisdom set things up, turn things around, reverse things, and usher people, positions, and places into His intended purpose—oftentimes without so much as our consent or acceptance.

This is because God doesn't need us as much as we may think He does. In His providence, He spoke through a donkey to prevent a prophet from placing a curse on His people (Num. 22:21–39). In His providence, He woke up a king in order to position Esther to save His people from annihilation (Esther 6:1). In His providence, He used marching around a wall by tired, hungry foot soldiers and priests to bring about one of the most amazing military feats of all time (Josh. 6:1–20). God's providence and His sovereign control exist, whether we acknowledge it or not. Thus, for each of us to discover the importance of working, living, and moving within it is one of the most critical life skills we could ever obtain.

However, unfortunately, this wisdom is often lost on our egos. Why? Because most people want to do what they want to do. Most people want to feel as if they are calling the shots. Most people want to be the center attraction in the three-ring circus known as their life. And so, what they must do in order to get rid of the truth of sovereignty in their own minds is to deny it, or rebel against it. Yet denying God's sovereignty or rebelling against His providence doesn't make it any less true. It just makes you or me feel like we have more control than we actually do.

In fact, rebellion against God is typically rooted in a desire to usurp His sovereignty. Yet because God is so good at being sovereign, He will often take someone's rejection of His sovereignty and make it work toward His sovereign purposes anyhow. He is so good at lining things up (especially when you don't want Him to be sovereign) that He winds up being sovereign over you not wanting Him to be sovereign as well!

Take Pharaoh, for example. God told Moses to tell Pharaoh to let His people go. That was His sovereign will. God sovereignly determined that His people would be free. Thus, He instructed the one who was holding them hostage to release them through His servant Moses. Yet time after time after time Pharaoh refused to cooperate with or surrender to God's will. In fact, Pharaoh became so entirely obstinate about the whole thing that he made God's people work even harder with less tools to get the work done. Not only did he refuse to let them go, but he also took them into a deeper level of bondage.

What did God do? God used Pharaoh's rebellion against His sovereign will to bring about His sovereign will. We discover this in Romans 9 where it says:

> What should we say then? Is there injustice with God? Absolutely not! For he tells Moses, "I will show mercy to whom I will show mercy, and I will have compassion on whom I will have compassion." So then, it does not depend on human will or effort but on God who shows mercy. For the Scripture tells Pharaoh, "I raised you up for this reason

so that I may display my power in you and that my name may be proclaimed in the whole earth." So then, he has mercy on whom he wants to have mercy and he hardens whom he wants to harden. (Rom. 9:14–18)

In this passage, it says that God Himself has the power to harden hearts. In Exodus 9:34–35, we gain a glimpse at this progression,

When Pharaoh saw that the rain, hail, and thunder had ceased, he sinned again and hardened his heart, he and his officials. So Pharaoh's heart was hard, and he did not let the Israelites go, as the LORD had said through Moses.

We see in these verses that Pharaoh became obstinate. His heart became rock solid, determined not to do what God was instructing him to do through His servant Moses. Pharaoh made it clear, in no uncertain terms, that he would not go along with God's will or align himself under God's rule. Thus, God answered Pharaoh with total agreement. God cooperated with Pharaoh's rebellion by making his rebellion even worse.

God took Pharaoh's hardened heart and made it coal.

As a result of God hardening Pharaoh's heart, when Pharaoh did eventually succumb to the plagues and the pressure put on him by God to release His people, this reversal produced even greater glory for God than it could have before. This is because as Pharaoh became drunk with rage, he made unwise decisions to chase after Moses and the Israelites in order to capture them and bring them back as slaves. Even though in a moment of weakness following the death of his son, Pharaoh had let the Israelites go, he quickly changed his mind and chased after them. His hardened heart refused to let go of his way, his power, and his preference. But because of the chase, God was able to display His way, His power, and the supremacy of His preference. Swallowing the Egyptian army in the heart of the Red Sea, God broadcast to those on hand, as well as those to come, that He was—and *is*—in charge. There would be no doubts as to who called the shots when the Egyptians could not escape God providentially swallowing them up whole.

Similarly, God will often allow things in our own lives to go south, or to remain unchanged, in order to bring us to a place where His sovereignty is on display. Whether it is our own hearts or someone else's, rebellion against God breeds further rebellion as the Lord uses those times and situations to demonstrate His sovereign hand.

Friend, the greatest truth you can ever know about God (next to hearing and receiving the message of salvation) is His sovereignty. Because when you know that God *is* in control—even of those things that appear to be out of control—you are able to move through life benefiting from the blessings of assurance, peace, and self-control. When you truly understand that He *is* in your corner—your greatest defender and vindicator—you will no longer seek to rescue yourself. It is only in drawing close to Him in such a way that you can hear Him and, as a result, follow Him that you will experience His deliverance in every area of your life.

Far too often, when we face a trial or adverse situation in life, we try to figure it out, fix it, logically argue our way through it, and more. Yet there is no logic or reason to having the Egyptians chase the Israelites into the separated waters of the Red Sea (Exod. 14:27–28). That is not a solution Moses could have contrived on his own. That is not a strategy any military general would have put into play.

Similarly, when you or I rely too much on our own reasoning, we leave ourselves vulnerable to what that reasoning will produce, rather than setting ourselves up for God's intervention instead.

God *is* in control.

And in case you read over that line too quickly, let me write it one more time: God *is* in control. It doesn't matter how things appear to you right now. It doesn't matter what authority you feel your boss has over you right now. It doesn't matter what that addiction is telling you to do, or that mate, or that mess you have found yourself in. None of those people or situations are in ultimate control.

Yes, they may look like they are. After all, Pharaoh had every appearance of control over the Israelites. Even as his army chased them across the wilderness and backed them up against an enormous body of water no one knew how they would go around. But what you see is never all there is to be seen. Sovereignty shapes water differently and sets souls free. Providence paves a way where there seemed to be no way at all. Sovereignty roars its authority so loudly that even your greatest threats must cower beneath the blast of its breath.

God *is* in control. Wisdom recognizes this reality and relinquishes the reins of self-preservation while grasping tightly to the yoke of His hope. Wrapping yourself in the truth of God's providential provision will help you to deal with life on good days and bad days. It is in knowing that God is in control that you get rid of the concepts of mistakes, luck, chance, or fate. It means you recognize that things are not random even if they look random. It means that the pathway you are on is leading somewhere with a purpose. It means you have hope.

> *Sovereignty roars its authority so loudly that even your greatest threats must cower beneath the blast of its breath.*

The sovereignty of God is so spectacular that He reigns even over the infinitesimal details while simultaneously keeping the stars, moon, and sun hanging in their places. If we could ever get this next verse in the depth of our psyche so much so that it gives birth to our beliefs, our lives would rid themselves of anxiety and grief. Psalm 115:3 tells us, "Our God is in heaven and does whatever he pleases." Essentially, God is in charge; He does whatever He wants to do.

God is so comprehensively, completely sovereign that He holds no checks and balances to keep Him slowed down. He has no bureaucracy and hoops to jump through in order to carry out His decisions. He sustains and develops that which He brings into existence.

In short, no one can stand in God's way. No one. Not even you. Not even me. Not even that enemy, compulsion, or circumstance that is seeking to take you down. Nothing can thwart God's plan because, as the Scripture says, He "does whatever he pleases" (Ps. 115:3).

Now, you can be on the good side of God's sovereignty or you can be on the bad side of God's sovereignty. That doesn't change His sovereignty. It just changes your personal experience of it. It's like when a parent tells a teenager, "We can make this easy or we can make it hard—that's up to you." Meaning: the teenager's choices will have an impact on how the parents go about teaching the lesson they are trying to convey. And while your actions never determine God's providence, your actions do influence how that providence comes to light in your life.

God's plans may be made manifest with your cooperation, or they may be made manifest in spite of your rebellion. Regardless, His pathways and plans will come about. God knows that whichever direction you go on the path He's placed before you, He will get you to His intended destination. Now, due to your own choices, that may mean delays and treacherous treks—or even, like Moses, the loss of realizing the experience of the dream (Deut. 34:4). But He will keep pointing you in the direction He desires until His sovereign rule is achieved.

Providence and Personal Responsibility

Now, this raises a big question regarding personal responsibility. Since God is sovereign and He does whatever He chooses to do, then it would be easy to assume that what I do does not matter. Resigning yourself to a worldview such as this is what we call "fatalism." Fatalism reflects a mind-set that distances personal choice from consequences. But fatalism is not biblical.

While Scripture teaches soundly on God's sovereignty, it also teaches that within God's sovereignty, our decisions are used as part of the movements in history. God doesn't dismiss what we do; He uses it.

Let me give you an example from one of my favorite sports—football. In football, there are sovereign guidelines the NFL has established within which all teams must operate. This declares and sets forth the overall structure of the game. Then, for each team there is also a large and detailed playbook outlining the various options a team can employ in order to score points in the game, or to try and keep the other team from scoring points.

While these things are all established, it is up to the individual coaches and players to decide what they are going to do on the field. There is freedom to operate within the rules and according to plays that propel a team forward, or there is freedom to operate outside the rules or with poor plays. Either way, the choices of the coaches and the team will have a direct impact on what happens next. If they choose to operate outside of the rules in any way, they will be penalized. And while it may have only been one player who broke the rule, the entire team will suffer the additional yardage or whatever resultant penalty may have come about.

In God's sovereignty, He has established boundaries within which we are to function. When we choose to go outside of those boundaries, He has also allowed consequences to come about which are tied to those choices. Well-executed plays within the structure and alignment of His rule come with good results as well. And while God has a preferred will for each of us, He also has an allowed will that adjusts based on the freedom He's granted us in our choices.

For example, God had called the Israelites out of slavery and into the Promised Land. He had even given them strong leaders such as Moses, Joshua, and Caleb who would take them into the battles they were to face. Yet because the Israelites chose to rebel against God and fear those around them in the land they were given, God allowed them to wander in the wilderness for another forty years before the next generation could enter into His preferred promise (Num. 32:13).

Blaming the devil comes about as a quick knee-jerk reaction when things start to deteriorate in our lives. It's easy to point the finger and assume it's spiritual warfare for each and every issue we face. But doing so negates a true comprehension of a principle found in Lamentations 3:37–38 which says:

Who is there who speaks and it happens, unless the Lord has ordained it? Do not both adversity and good come from the mouth of the Most High?

It is both adversity and good that come from the Lord, and these are largely dependent upon our own choices. It was not Satan that kept the Israelites wandering in the wilderness for forty years. It was God. What's more—it was the Israelites themselves, through their rebellion against His rightful rule in their lives. While God does not create nor condone sin and disobedience, He did create human freedom which allows people to choose sin and, therefore, bear its consequences.

A correct view of God's providential hand will increase our fear and reverence for Him rather than reduce it. This is because it is in understanding sovereignty that we come face-to-face with His holiness, and His loyalty to His own holiness and rule. While God's love is higher, wider, and deeper than anything you or I have ever known, His commitment to His own rule as King over all has created boundaries in which we are to experience that love.

The Purpose of Difficult Paths

God will also often use negative situations in life in order to develop within His children a greater resolve, refinement, and maturity (James 1:3; Rom. 5:4). Whenever sovereignty allows something that is not pleasant, always remember that it is also not random. It was allowed for a reason. God always has a reason for what He does, or for what He allows. As Lamentations 3:32 tells us, "For if He causes grief, then He will have compassion according to His abundant lovingkindness" (NASB).

We can understand this passage better when we reflect on it through the lens of a parent. If you are a parent and have ever disciplined one of your children, you know that the grief caused in the method of discipline was not intended for the purpose of hurting your child. If your child was grounded from attending any fun activities due to disobedience to you, you chose that form of punishment in order to teach your child a greater lesson. This greater lesson was also sought out with the intention of it keeping your child from future harm. The discipline was necessary for the growth. And while discipline is never fun, loving parents will always follow it up with compassion.

Similarly, God does not discipline us out of a spirit of meanness or malice. His discipline of His children comes couched with compassion and the desire for us to mature to such a degree that we keep from needing further discipline in the future.

Understanding this concept of sovereignty will solve a very big issue for you, and for most people. It is the issue of trust.

It is difficult to trust God when or if you do not believe He is sovereign. When things happen in your life that are painful or seem confusing, it is easy to lose trust in God's control and His goodness when you do not fully grasp His sovereignty. But once you grab this truth and hold onto it tightly—the truth that He is ruler, controller, sustainer, and authority over all—then the seemingly disconnected happenings of life are woven together into a tapestry of His perfect timing. The meanderings which seem to take you from place to place on the pathway of your days now lead somewhere.

And while you may not see the destination or be instantly relieved of the difficulties, your trust in His providential care and sovereign rule will give you the ability to rest rather than fret, be still rather than be anxious, or even praise rather than complain.

When you understand His sovereignty in the midst of not understanding what He is doing right then, you will learn how to see God in a way you've never seen Him before. You will discover the power of His presence and the purpose of His plans. You, as we are about to discover in diving into the story and saga of Esther, will come to experience the great reversal of people, plans, decrees, and seasons in which all once appeared lost.

CHAPTER THREE

Enter Esther

One day a very lonely frog went to a fortune-teller to see what his fortune would be. The fortune-teller told the lonely frog, "Don't worry because soon you are going to meet a girl who will want to know everything about you." The frog instantly got his hopes up. So the fortune-teller continued, "She's really, really going to want to know everything."

The frog was so excited to hear that he was going to meet a girl who wanted to know so much about him, so he asked the fortune-teller another question, "When will I meet her?"

That's when the fortune-teller responded promptly, "Next week in Biology class!"

Can you identify with this situation? Well, maybe not with the frog or biology class directly, but many of us can identify with how life can seem to be going really well one moment only to take an abrupt turn for the worse on the next. Sometimes, if the truth were told, we may feel as if our dreams are finally taking place only to discover that disaster follows them like a shadow.

It's in scenarios like these that we may question whether or not God even knows what He is doing. We also may assume that if we ourselves had the option of "being God," we certainly wouldn't be allowing what He appears to be allowing in our lives.

I'm sure Esther probably felt the same way at some point in her saga. After all, in one moment she became the queen over nearly everything. Then not much later, she faced the potential of losing nearly everything—even up to her own life—as her people were earmarked for execution.

But I'm getting ahead of myself in the telling of Esther's story. So let's slow down and start before the beginning. Doing so will give us the context in which we can understand and appreciate God's providential moves—not only in Esther's life, but also as these principles transcend into our own.

The Backstory

The curtain rises on Esther's story, as is the case with many other epic stories, with the central figure of a king. This king's kingdom stretched from Ethiopia to India, including 127 provinces. As you might imagine, this king wielded an enormous amount of power. They called him Xerxes. Xerxes sounds like it could be a character in a Marvel superhero film. He certainly lived the lifestyle of someone with superpowers. Like most superheroes, he also came with a second name: Ahasuerus. This was his title. And still others knew him by another title: *Shahanshah*, which literally translates as "king of kings." Depending on who was talking to him, or about him, would determine which name was used.

Yet, regardless of which name was used, his reign sat secure and supreme, situated within the borders of another familiar biblical account. Two familiar biblical accounts, actually. Those of Ezra and Nehemiah.

As in many movies or stage plays, scenes are inserted near the start to provide the audience with what is known as the "backstory." This backstory nearly always includes what is known as "foreshadowing." It is here where we uncover the motives behind the characters in the story. It is here where we discover why the conflict we are about to witness even winds up taking place. It is here where our hearts and souls are enlightened as to who is good and who represents evil, and why the two clash.

Esther's story has a significant backstory as well. During the time of Esther and her king, God was busy working with His people, the Israelites, to usher them back into the place of promise He had given them years before. The Israelites had been removed from this place previously due to their own sins and resultant consequences. Yet when those consequences had run their course, God moved in the hearts of two men named Ezra and Nehemiah to restore what sin had stolen. He began this by instructing the Israelites to return to Jerusalem and rebuild His temple, as recorded in Ezra 1:2, and taking place in the year 538 BC. This occurred during the reign of Cyrus, the first Persian king. To put it on the time line of Esther, Esther came to power as queen in 478 BC (roughly sixty years following God's first instructions to rebuild the temple).

Who is King Cyrus and how does he relate to Esther? Well, King Cyrus's daughter Atossa, along with her husband, Darius, later gave birth to a son. They named their son Xerxes. Thus, King Cyrus was King Xerxes' grandfather.

Esther's king had been born into royalty. But before any assumptions are made about what that means, let me explain that he had been born into a royal legacy unlike many ruling powers of that day. King Cyrus (his grandfather) and King Darius (his father) were both revered for ruling with a bent toward humanitarian and religious freedoms unique for that period of time.

Cultures in that day normalized both slavery and the subjection of humans, particularly following a national conquest. Yet "Cyrus the Great" set in order a law to ensure freedom of faith and the abolishment of slavery as well as forced-labor services. This reformative act known today as the *Cyrus Cylinder* is one of the first historical human rights declarations.

These two kings who reigned before Xerxes had a reputation for ruling more fairly and justly than any kings had ever done. Their power was great. Their wealth immense. And their pride certainly matched. But, for some reason in God's providential setting of the stage, these kings' hearts beat somewhat sympathetically toward those who were normally oppressed (Prov. 21:1).

Xerxes had big shoes to fill, having been birthed into a legacy of ruling well. He had risen to power during this season in which Persian royalty had enabled the Jews to restore the house of the Lord and return to their land.

By the time Xerxes secured full power, though, the relationship between the Persians and the Jews had become increasingly strained. His own thirst for power contributed to this. Cyrus's friends were Xerxes' enemies. For example, while Cyrus had been a friend to enemies such as Babylon in his time, Xerxes reversed the relationship and subjugated them instead. He tore down their golden statues, melting them for all to see. Xerxes positioned himself to be the one and only rule. He showed no mercy. He extended no grace. His heart beat to the drum of total dominion, seeking to conquer and exploit all within reach.

But not only did Xerxes reverse the nature of the external relationships outside Persian culture which had once been cultivated by his grandfather and father, his reputation for fierce rule was also felt within his own domain. The story is told of one of his leaders named Pythias (a descendant of a king himself) who once received a bad omen about an upcoming battle which Xerxes had demanded that all able-bodied men take part in. Pythias felt that the battle was unwinnable and that he risked losing all five of his sons in the defeat. Thus, he inquired of the king if his oldest son might be spared from entrance into the fight. In this manner, Pythias might retain one of his sons in order to provide him with an heir, as well as someone to take care of him in his old age.

Xerxes' response echoed far and wide, dismantling the trust of all under his rule while replacing it with nothing but sheer fear. Rather than allow Pythias's oldest son to be exempt from the battle, Xerxes ordered that his oldest son be cut in two. Then he had one section of his corpse placed on each side of the road upon which his army, including Pythias and his remaining four sons, would march on as they headed into war.

Esther's king was no pushover. Xerxes was a king to be feared, and for good reason. Thus, while the Jews had received some level of lenience from Cyrus and Darius previously, those living during Xerxes' reign would not have looked to him for the same.

For Such a Time Beyond This

Much of this hatred toward the Jews was rooted in a shared history of battles, conquering, and a blood-thirst for power. Understanding Esther's story beyond the chapters that encase her most famous exploits and gains is critical to understanding God's providence. As Daniel 2:21 tells us, "He changes the times and seasons; he removes kings and establishes kings." It is God who works things together outside of time, transcending generations and surpassing seasons which had once seemingly been set in stone. God's providential pathways zig-zag through a multitude of people, places, and purposes in order to intersect for His intended aim.

Through a series of sovereign twists and turns, Esther's influence with the king led to much more than many people give her credit for in contemporary reflection. While she is known as the queen who found courage to stand up for her people "for such a time as this" (Esther 4:14), her impact stretched beyond what most of us may know. Yes, she empowered her people to defend themselves against a ploy to wipe them out entirely (as we will see as we journey through her story). But her influence went beyond the palace. It went beyond the parties and banquets. It went beyond the celebration she later established called Purim. It went beyond the pages of the biblical book in her name.

Esther's impact extended to Jerusalem itself.

While the rebuilding of the Jerusalem walls is nearly always attributed to Nehemiah (444 BC)—who came after Esther in linear time lines (Esther enters as queen in 478 BC)—this community-restoration success may be just as much Esther's legacy as Nehemiah's. How so? It was during the reign of Artaxerxes, the son of Xerxes (Esther's king), that Ezra was commissioned to dedicate the temple (Ezra 7:11–26) for the Jews. It is also around this same time that Nehemiah was being prepared by the Lord to return to the land in order to establish the pathway for its eventual re-habitation.

The Israelites' pathway home began when Nehemiah, who served as the cupbearer to King Artaxerxes, appeared solemn and gloomy in his presence. Inquiring as to why his cupbearer lacked his normal vitality, the king received his answer when Nehemiah told him that his heart broke over the displacement of his people and the destruction of their land (Neh. 2:1–3).

King Artaxerxes was then moved with compassion for what Nehemiah told him, so he asked him what he would need in order to help his people return to their land. An intricate plan for rebuilding and restoration was created and, long story short, the king not only let one of his most trusted servants go (a cupbearer literally held the king's life in his own hands), but the king also funded the rebuilding plan for a people many considered to be a potential enemy.

If you read over that narrative too quickly or simply view the flannel board presentation of the facts, it may never hit you as odd that a king would be moved to do so much for a people who didn't officially belong to him. Especially a king who followed a predecessor hell-bent on exploiting and destroying people groups far and wide.

But that's why Nehemiah 2:6 is so critical. This verse gives us a peek into what may have influenced such a kind and generous response from the king of Persia toward the Jews. We read:

> The king, with the queen sitting beside him, asked me [Nehemiah], "How long will your journey take, and when will you return?" So I gave him a definite time, and it pleased the king to send me.

As we see in this verse, the king hadn't been alone when he talked with Nehemiah. The passage tells us that there was a queen sitting beside him. And while we don't know exactly who that queen was, by the nature of his gracious response toward the Jews, we can gain some insight.

Royal culture in Persia permitted kings to have many wives and women during their reign; however, they typically chose one woman for the role of "chief wife," otherwise known as queen. In many cases, if a king died and his son took the throne, and the first king's wife was still alive, she took the role of "Queen Mother." Most biblical historians assert that the queen who sat with Artaxerxes during this conversation with Nehemiah was Damaspia, yet there are a few who will purport that it could have even been Esther, now functioning as the Queen Mother. Either way, Esther's prominent influence toward the Jewish people undoubtedly lingered through-out the halls, hearts, and crevices of this great empire. Whether it was her whispering in the king's ear or her mentoring the queen who had followed her, the atmosphere of compassion toward the Jews had been restored.

Power and impact don't always come through direct decree. In fact, it is often the voice no one else hears that guides the voice all do. Not only did this king provide the funds to begin the rebuild-ing of Jerusalem, not only did he provide Nehemiah with a leave-of-absence to oversee it, but he also provided protection against anyone who would stand in the way. This is in stark contrast to his predecessor's reign and no doubt a direct link to Queen Esther's presence.

Whatever the path looked like in getting to this point in the palace culture, Esther's life and legacy had led to an atmosphere of favor toward a group of people who could have easily been wiped out by the Persians, or continually subjugated under their rule.

From Parties to Purim

Superhero movies, similar in many ways to the true saga of Esther, often include the backstory of fathers, grandfathers, or ancestors because knowing the DNA of a person, as well as his or her history, fleshes out the current characters all the more. Knowing the time period also provides context. The book of Esther fits chronologically between chapters 6 and 7 of the book of Ezra. Reading all three books of Esther, Ezra, and Nehemiah helps paint the historical picture all the more.

The book of Esther itself begins with a party. The curtains rise on a king throwing a party. The stage is covered with people laughing, dancing, drinking, eating, and entertaining each other. This isn't your ordinary party, after all. This is a party by King Xerxes. This is a party thrown by a king who is a legend among kings. A militant leader over a military of millions, you may know Xerxes best for his one loss rather than his multiple wins. You may know him best for his insatiable ego rather than his strategic prowess.

Having conquered lands, nations, and people, having annihilated his enemies brutally, inhumanely, and decisively, he may still be best remembered for a battle against only a few. The official name of the fight was the Battle of Thermopylae. Most people, though, know it simply as the 300.

In 480 BC, 300 Spartans stopped a blood-hungry king from moving forward to overtake Greece. In the theatrical retelling of this epic clash we see in the movie *300*, we get a peek into Xerxes' conceit. And while what was said in the film may not have been said precisely in real life, the overarching sentiment it portrays holds true to historical recordings about this man and his quest for overpowering others. In the film, Xerxes looks to the commander of his enemies and asks for only one thing—ironically enough, the very same thing Haman will later ask of Mordecai in the story of Esther.

King Xerxes says, "Leonides would have you stand. All I ask is that you kneel."

If you know history at all, or if you have seen the film *300*, you know that kneeling was not an option for the Spartans. They refused to bow to the Persians, even if it meant their lives. Rather, they rose up and carried out one of the greatest military defeats in recorded history. Xerxes and his deflated army later returned to Persia, nursing not only their flesh wounds but also a collectively wounded psyche.

But just a few years before the battle with the three hundred Spartans took place, before the invasion of Greece, and before Xerxes' god-like status became challenged at all, he did what most kings do. He threw a party. Scripture tells us this was a spectacular party. It was also a costly party. And a long party. This party lasted six entire months.

This unusual party, as well as the subsequent after-party lasting seven days, is best described in the Bible's retelling of it:

> He displayed the glorious wealth of his kingdom and the magnificent splendor of his greatness for a total of 180 days.
>
> At the end of this time, the king held a week-long banquet in the garden courtyard of the royal palace for all the people, from the greatest to the least, who were present in the fortress of Susa. White and violet linen hangings were fastened with fine white and purple linen cords to silver rods on marble columns. Gold and silver couches were arranged on a mosaic pavement of red feldspar, marble, mother-of-pearl, and precious stones.
>
> Drinks were served in an array of gold goblets, each with a different design. Royal wine flowed freely, according to the king's bounty. The drinking was according to royal decree: "There are no restrictions." The king had ordered every wine steward in his household to serve whatever each person wanted. Queen Vashti also gave a feast for the women of King Ahasuerus's palace. (Esther 1:4–9)

In summary, the king held nothing back from this party. For 180 days, he displayed the might, glory, and power of his kingdom to all who could see. Then, to top it off, just following the six-month celebration, the king and the queen threw two separate seven-day parties for the cream of the crop. The men partied in one location while the women partied in another.

At the conclusion of this seven-day celebration, something providential took place. The king was drunk. Or, as the Bible says, he was "merry with wine" (Esther 1:10 NASB). In that state of mind, he commanded his leaders to bring his queen Vashti and to parade her in front of the men who had partied with him in order to display her beauty. Basically, he wanted her to strut her stuff in front of his posse. He wanted to show her off.

But the queen refused. Doubtless, she had suffered much under her cruel husband, but this time, in her dignity, she refused to be his show-and-tell. In her dignity, she said no.

Saying "no" to a king can come with consequences. Especially this king. As a result of her refusal, the king now faced a dilemma. His friends urged him to ban her and revoke her title because they feared their wives would rebel based on her example. We read what they said:

> "For the queen's action will become public knowledge to all the women and cause them to despise their husbands and say, 'King Ahasuerus ordered Queen Vashti brought before him, but she did not come.' Before this day is over, the noble women of Persia and Media who hear about the queen's act will say the same thing to all the king's officials, resulting in more contempt and fury.

"If it meets the king's approval, he should personally issue a royal decree. Let it be recorded in the laws of Persia and Media, so that it cannot be revoked: Vashti is not to enter King Ahasuerus's presence, and her royal position is to be given to another woman who is more worthy than she." (Esther 1:17–19)

Essentially, they told him they didn't need any more rebellious and independent women in the kingdom. He agreed. Thus, the king banned Vashti from being his queen.

Some time passed between the king revoking Queen Vashti's title and the entrance of Esther on the stage. In fact, four years passed before the king's anger toward Vashti subsided. It could be that the king had suffered a crack in his armor. It was in this four-year period that the failed invasion of Greece and humiliating defeat at the hands of the Spartans took place. No doubt, his ego took a hit. Whatever led to it, the king became depressed. We know this because the second chapter in the book of Esther opens with the king's attendants suggesting that he hold a beauty contest of sorts in order to "audition" a new queen for him. They were seeking to cheer him up. To do so, they suggested that every beautiful virgin be brought to him in order for him to scout out the best choice for his new queen. They must have assumed this could lift his spirits.

The whole thing sounded intriguing to the king, so the search began. An elaborate plan of locating women, preparing them through a season of oils and perfumes, and then auditioning them, so to speak, through each having a night with the king had unfolded.

Cue Esther.

Esther, also known as Hadassah (a name which means "myrtle") had no mother or father. She had been orphaned along the way and her cousin Mordecai had chosen to raise her. Perhaps he was the one who gave her the name Esther, which means *star*, in remembrance of her parents. We don't know for sure. But what we do know is that the Scripture tells us Mordecai took her in as if she was his own daughter (Esther 2:7).

Scripture also tells us that Esther was a very attractive woman. She is described as "beautiful of form and face." Esther's beauty got her noticed, of course, and she was chosen to be one of the women who would be placed on the path to become queen. Yet while her beauty may have gotten her noticed, there was something else about her that kept her noticed. As the R&B group The Temptations' song goes, "beauty is only skin deep." Looks may turn heads but looks alone won't make those turned heads stay. It takes more than that. Esther possessed an additional special quality—we may call it today things like charisma, poise, presence, or authenticity. Whatever it was, it evoked something longer than just a look. In fact, we are told she found "favor" with the person in charge of all of the women. And that favor wound up giving her an advantage with the king. We read:

> When the king's command and edict became public knowledge and when many young women were gathered at the

fortress of Susa under Hegai's supervision, Esther was taken to the palace, into the supervision of Hegai, keeper of the women. The young woman pleased him and gained his favor so that he accelerated the process of the beauty treatments and the special diet that she received. He assigned seven hand-picked female servants to her from the palace and transferred her and her servants to the harem's best quarters. (Esther 2:8–9)

The favor Esther found opened doors for her to have seven maids, choice food, and cosmetics given to her. It also had her placed in the best place to live as she prepared to meet the king. But not only did Esther have great looks and a special quality to her, she also had wisdom. She was wise enough to listen to her cousin Mordecai and not share with anyone about her Jewish heritage. She was wise enough to follow his leading in her life as they both sought this position of influence for her. Knowing this was their opportunity, Mordecai stayed close by.

Every day, the Scripture tells us, Mordecai would pace outside near the gates and doors of where Esther stayed in order to hear word on how she was doing and how her status fared (Esther 2:11). And every day he would undoubtedly hear something along the lines of, "Not yet." Until the day finally came when it was Esther's turn to spend a night with the king.

The way the search had been set up, each woman would have twelve months of preparation before her time with the king. At the end of those twelve months, she would get one night to make a lasting impression. She was also allowed to bring with her anything she wanted to help make that night more memorable. What's more, it's likely she got to keep the things she brought with her, when the night was over. Some may have considered it an opportunity to get something for themselves out of the deal. We read:

> When the young woman would go to the king, she was given whatever she requested to take with her from the harem to the palace. She would go in the evening, and in the morning she would return to a second harem under the supervision of the king's eunuch Shaashgaz, keeper of the concubines. She never went to the king again, unless he desired her and summoned her by name. (Esther 2:13–14)

The women were given anything they desired from the palace. The transition would occur from the first harem where each woman was a virgin. Then they would spend a night with the king and afterwards be placed in the second harem, where each woman was no longer a virgin. This can also be known as a concubine. Each woman could be summoned again from the second harem, but only if the king asked for her by name.

As you might imagine, a night with the king wasn't a night playing Scrabble. It was a night of sex, outside of the confines of marriage. Which brings up an interesting point. Adultery and fornication were prohibited in God's law. In addition, Jews were prohibited from marrying pagans (Deut. 7:1–4). And yet here was Esther providentially positioned to do just that. And while God's name does not appear anywhere in the book, He is still the Puppet-Master working things out behind the scenes. So, you've got this happening outside of God's ideal, prescribed ways, and yet it is still happening. Which is a reminder that we can never box God into our way of thinking. His providence allows, or causes, the good, the bad, and the ugly to work together toward His intended aim.

It's important to remember here that for God, the ends justify the means. He is moving everything toward His end, and He gets there in mysterious ways. But the ends justify the means for Him because He is all-knowing and all-wise. We are not all-knowing and all-wise. All we have is the Word He has given us in the Bible. Thus, the fact that God allows and uses the good, bad, and ugly to work toward His end does not give us license to disobey His commands in the hopes that the end will make it worth it. God is God, and He alone has this wisdom. We are called to obey.

Esther knew that. Esther trusted that. She also knew this was her one opportunity to enter a higher status in life than she and her family had ever known. Yes, she was beautiful. But we are told that all the women who were chosen to audition for this role were beautiful. It would take more than looks to secure the crown. That's why Esther remained close to the king's eunuch, the one with whom she had found favor. If anyone knew the king's likes or dislikes, it would be him. Thus, when it was time for Esther to enter the king's bed chambers, she took only what Hegai advised. It says:

Esther was the daughter of Abihail, the uncle of Mordecai who had adopted her as his own daughter. When her turn came to go to the king, she did not ask for anything except what Hegai, the king's eunuch, keeper of the women, suggested. Esther gained favor in the eyes of everyone who saw her.

She was taken to King Ahasuerus in the palace in the tenth month, the month Tebeth, in the seventh year of his reign. The king loved Esther more than all the other women. She won more favor and approval from him than did any of the other virgins. He placed the royal crown on her head and made her queen in place of Vashti. (Esther 2:15–17)

Why did the king love Esther more than all the other women? Why did Esther find favor with him similar to how she had found favor with his eunuch a year earlier? The narrative recorded in Scripture doesn't state it explicitly, but we can conjecture through what we have been told. You'll notice that all of the other women took in whatever they wanted from the first harem. Whatever they took in was then removed from the king's chambers the next day and went with them to the second harem. Otherwise, the items would have simply piled up in the king's room. After a year of preparation, this was their opportunity to secure for themselves a little something-something on the side. Yet when Esther entered the presence of the king, she took nothing other than what the eunuch advised.

You need to keep in mind that when you are a king, you don't know who to trust. When you are a king, you don't know who is real and authentic. You don't know who wants you versus who just wants your stuff. Who wants you or who just wants to ride in your chariot. Who wants you or who wants a closet in the palace filled with fine linens and trinkets.

The point that the author of the book of Esther emphasizes is that Esther wasn't like the other women. Esther didn't ask for anything. She was not trying to be a drifter or an opportunist in order to get all she could. She wasn't trying to play the king. Rather, she was trying to win him. There's an enormous difference between the two.

The king knew that too. So he made her his queen.

Esther had something different about her. Something special. She didn't run out and put "for such a time as this" bumper stickers all over her chariots. She didn't take her role for granted, nor did she take it lightly. Esther knew that the favor she had found could be removed just as fast as it had been given. She also knew that beauty doesn't last forever, and crowns can come off just as easily as polish on nails. No, Esther thought long-term. Her face was beautiful but her mind was strategic and her heart was humble.

That's why not long after she became queen, she did the right thing in the face of grave danger. While sitting at the king's gate, Mordecai had uncovered a plot between some angry citizens who were looking to kill the king. It was an assassination plot. When Mordecai informed Esther, Esther informed the king. She risked her reputation on the reliability of her cousin. Esther hadn't heard the plot herself. Esther knew there would be an investigation to see whether or not it was true. But Esther demonstrated her own loyalty to the king and to his longevity by letting him in on the plan. The plot was then searched out and found to be valid. Both men were hanged on the gallows and the incident was recorded in the Historical Record (Esther 2:23). This Historical Record would later prove to be key in God's providential tweaking and turning in His ultimate deliverance of His people from a twisted plot.

Mordecai's name wound up being written in this book, a book which the king later had read to him on a night when he could not sleep. Mordecai's name was written in it because he had been situated at a gate near a palace where his family member was now queen. Because he had been situated at the gate, he had overheard a conversation about a plan to assassinate the king. You see, when the Puppet-Master moves behind the scenes of our lives, even though you may not see Him or His name may not be made known, He is always doing something bigger than what you or I can see. You need to trust Him where you are. He's the only One who can take a mess and make a miracle. That's why the phrase "the devil is in the details" is not entirely accurate. Because once you understand the providence of God, you'll know that God is in the details all the more. As we see, He's positioned Esther with favor in order to afford her a role of influence when it will matter most.

> *He is always doing something bigger than what you or I can see.*

God has positioned you where you are as well. It may not make sense to you right now. But if you will learn to trust His heart even when you cannot spot His hand, you will discover—like Esther—that He knows the path you are taking and how to get you where He wants you to be so that you can fulfill your greatest level of kingdom impact in your own legacy.

CHAPTER FOUR

The Prerequisites of Purpose

 Many Christians will have spent a large part of their lives climbing the ladder of success only to discover at the end that it was leaning against the wrong wall. In an effort to meet the standards of our world's system as well as what our world calls "success," many people will have missed the purposes of God. They may have wound up being great in their careers, education, and bank accounts, but will stand before God never having finished the work that He created them to do. They will not have lived out their purpose, destiny, or their divinely designed reason for being.

Yet one of the reasons we are not raptured at the moment of conversion is because God left us here for the achievement and the accomplishment of a kingdom-purpose. Unfortunately today, it's very easy to get caught up in the wrong quest. While this can include the pursuit of people, possessions, paychecks, power, popularity—and perhaps even some piety sprinkled in there to make us feel better—when what we do is not tied to the kingdom and God's overarching agenda, we've missed the mark.

As we are walking along the pathway of a woman's life named Esther, we are discovering that God's fingerprints appear everywhere. We've seen how He can take a young, orphaned girl and cause her to ascend to royalty. A slave can become a queen. The beauty God gave her in both form and face caught the king's servant's attention, which then encouraged him to help her in preparations for approaching the king. To say that Esther had moved up the ladder of success would be an understatement. She was the picture of success, a personal portrait of providential favor.

We pick up Esther's story where we left off, and she has entered a season of glory, power, and exalted position. This was her time. This was her moment. In just a few short flips of the pages in her life, we discover she has made it on the world's stage in every way.

It's common for people to talk about "making it" or it being their "season" or their "time." Maybe you've said things of that nature as well. When life starts clicking on all four cylinders, it's easy to toss your head back with a hearty laugh in an affirmation of success. And while it's easy to draw that conclusion about our lives, how do we really know when God has prepared us for our season? How do we really know when it's our time—that period in history where God has worked the good, the bad, and the ugly all together in order to bring you to a space of usefulness for His kingdom agenda?

The answer to this question might surprise you. Oftentimes, we can confirm it is our season to be used mightily by God when we face a dilemma, or an issue, that we don't quite know how to face on our own. Our "season" does not boil down to those moments where blessings rain down and all in life goes well. No, our "season" comes when our usefulness for the kingdom matches our calling. In fact, a person's "season" is often preceded by a deluge of testing. This is exactly what happened to Queen Esther at the beginning of Esther chapter 3.

> *How do we really know when God has prepared us for our season?*

In the first few verses of this chapter, we learn of the king promoting a man named Haman and advancing him by establishing his authority over all the princes who were with him. As a result of this promotion, every servant of the king was to bow and pay homage to Haman. After all, Haman was now the second most powerful person in the Medo-Persian Empire. Due to his role, the king had decreed that he wanted public recognition of his promotion through an outward display of humility and honor through the form of bowing.

Immediately, everyone began to bow before Haman. Everyone, that is, except for Queen Esther's cousin Mordecai. Whenever Haman would pass through the city gates, people everywhere would take their position of servitude and bow. Yet Mordecai refused. Mordecai linked the act of bowing and paying homage with that of offering worship, which would be idolatry. And while he could respect Haman's role and position over him, he could not worship Haman. Mordecai reserved worship for God, and God alone.

In Esther 3:3, we read the response Mordecai faced as a result of his decision: "The members of the royal staff at the King's Gate asked Mordecai, 'Why are you disobeying the king's command?'"

So persistent were Haman's servants that they spoke to Mordecai daily concerning his refusal to bow. They gave him every chance in the world to get in alignment underneath the governmental decree to bow before the second-in-command. When Mordecai would not respond in the method they wanted, they took their complaint up the ladder straight to Haman himself.

Haman didn't take too highly to Mordecai's dismissal of his personal esteem and honor. In fact, we read in Esther 3:5 that Mordecai's refusal filled him with hate. Haman, like the king he served who had demanded the three hundred Spartans to kneel before him, thrived on power. He "was filled with rage." So much so, that he determined to not only kill Mordecai himself but to also kill all of Mordecai's people, the Jews.

Haman's pride led him to make a decision of genocide against an entire group of people living within his domain. The failure by one man to recognize his clout led him to seek to kill an entire population.

As we've seen, though, Haman's hate wasn't solely rooted in Mordecai's lack of honor. There was a history between the Jews and Persians, a history of violence, war, and division. Mordecai simply triggered a centuries-long feud, fueling this power-hungry politician.

Bringing the idea of getting rid of the Jews to the king, Haman reworded the issue at hand to cause it to appear more so as a slight against the king's rule and authority than as a dismissal of Haman himself. Haman hadn't risen to power through diligence alone. This subtle manipulation of the problem dug deep into the king's heart when Haman explained:

> Then Haman informed King Ahasuerus, "There is one ethnic group, scattered throughout the peoples in every province of your kingdom, keeping themselves separate. Their laws are different from everyone else's and they do not obey the king's laws. It is not in the king's best interest to tolerate them. If the king approves, let an order be drawn up authorizing their destruction, and I will pay 375 tons of silver to the officials for deposit in the royal treasury." (Esther 3:8–9)

You'll notice there is no mention of Mordecai. No mention of Haman's lack of being honored. Rather, Haman deviously sought to destroy the Jews by not only pitting them entirely against the king's laws and his interests, but also by offering to pay a reward for their annihilation. The next verse gives us the king's response but it also points out a critical element of the background in this story. It says, "The king removed his signet ring from his finger and gave it to Haman son of Hammedatha the Agagite, the enemy of the Jewish people" (v. 10).

Haman is an Agagite. In fact, that point shouldn't go unnoticed because we're told a couple of times in the book of Esther that he is an Agagite. Now, that may not mean much to you, but God doesn't waste His words. This fact has a history behind it.

See, the Agagites came from a place called Agag. Agag is found in Scripture in 1 Samuel 15:1–23. To summarize it, Agag is head of the Amalekites, and the Amalekites were trying to destroy the Jews long before Haman came onto the scene. Many years prior, when Saul was king, God told Saul:

> "This is what the LORD of Armies says: 'I witnessed what the Amalekites did to the Israelites when they opposed them along the way as they were coming out of Egypt. Now go and attack the Amalekites and completely destroy everything they have. Do not spare them. Kill men and women, infants and nursing babies, oxen and sheep, camels and donkeys.'" (1 Sam. 15:2–3)

God made it inextricably clear that He wanted King Saul to wipe out the Amalekites because of what they had done to His nation of Israel and what they had the potential to do should they be allowed to move forward in strength. But Saul thought he was too smart for God and thus he decided not to kill the king. Instead of obeying God completely, Saul offered up only partial obedience—which is, in all actuality, complete disobedience. King Agag was allowed to live, resulting in a legacy pitted fiercely against the Jews. This is where we find ourselves in the book of Esther, at a time when the fruit of the root that had not been dealt with entirely earlier is rearing its vicious head against the Israelites once again.

The principle back then remains the principle today. It is in those times when we offer God only partial obedience that we allow the fruit of our unaddressed sin to linger in our lives and circumstances much longer than it ever should. When you or I fail to fully deal with something that God told us to deal with long ago, we will continue to face the repercussions from it.

The entire race of Jews faced extermination at the hands and heart of an enemy from years gone by. Haman's hatred was wrapped up in more than just a lack of honor on behalf of Mordecai. Haman's hatred came coupled with vengeance and reprisal. His hatred stirred on behalf of the blood of his ancestors. His thirst for power over the Jews didn't merely arise out of the risen stature of Mordecai. Rather, it went decades deep into a history rife with racial conflict. But had Saul, the leader of God's people Israel, been obedient to God's commands, Haman never would have been on the scene threatening to destroy the Jews.

Thus, his plot and ploy to rid his nation of the Jews was set in stone, or—as it were—in the king's signet ring. The king had agreed and now Esther and her people were on the pathway to total annihilation.

Which brings us to another critical principle on how to discern if it's your time—your *season*. You know it's your time when God connects spiritual preparation with spiritual warfare. You see, Haman was an agent of the devil whose goal was to thwart the purposes of God on earth. In the Old Testament, this goal was carried out primarily through the targeting and destruction of the Jewish people, seeing as that was through whom the Messiah had been chosen to come. In the New Testament as well as in the age in which we live, this goal has to do with the muting of the effectiveness of the church as well as the people who serve as representatives of God.

> *You know it's your time when God connects spiritual preparation with spiritual warfare.*

In order to pull off this goal, Satan uses people and systems to seek to destroy the program, promises, and purposes of God. In the time of Esther, this focus revolved around the Jewish people. God had said that He would build this group of people, establish and protect them because they were going to be His people through whom the Messiah would come. Thus, all along the way in the history of the Jewish culture, there is a pattern of genocide and destruction. This is because whenever God is getting ready to use someone—or a group of individuals—there will be battles to overcome. They will have to face spiritual opposition. Satan's main focus is seeking to destroy God's program and purpose in the lives of those who are called to serve God.

See, your life is not just about you. It's about the greater plan God has, of which you are a part. Getting rid of Mordecai wasn't just about getting rid of Mordecai. It was a tool in the hands of Satan used to set in motion a play to remove an entire people—the people through whom Jesus would later come—from the planet.

Spiritual battles occur on the pathways to purpose because there is an enemy lurking on this same pathway, and he wants nothing more than to stop you in your tracks.

Before David could ever be recognized as the future king of Israel, he had to go to battle first. He had to face Goliath. It wasn't until he defeated Goliath that he began to emerge in the preparation for kingship. Prior to God elevating him to his ultimate purpose, God allowed him to go through a spiritual battle.

Spiritual warfare is always a prerequisite to spiritual purpose. If you are not willing to demonstrate that you are able to deal with the spiritual issues that Satan brings in your life aimed at thwarting God's purpose in your life, then you are not ready to realize your ultimate spiritual destiny. What God wants to know before He gives you spiritual responsibility is that He can trust you to have the wisdom and self-restraint to use the spiritual weapons of warfare when the going gets tough. He wants to know that the spiritual won't be thrown aside when the natural issues of life show up. It's really easy when challenges come your way to start relying on what you know to do in the natural realm. It's easy to go secular and leave the spiritual at bay when pathways diverge into darkness. It's only when you have demonstrated a reliance on spiritual weapons for spiritual battles that God is going to release you for your time, your season—your ultimate purpose in life.

Mordecai had demonstrated loyalty and commitment in the face of persecution. He had demonstrated loyalty and commitment in raising and advising Esther this far. As a result, the stage was set for one of the greatest spiritual battles of all time. But there would be a gap first.

According to verses twelve and thirteen, the king's scribes gathered on the thirteenth day of the first month in order to alert the Jews by letter and courier that the king planned to have his army kill and annihilate them on the thirteenth day of the twelfth month, and to seize their possessions as plunder. There is an eleven-month window between the time of declaration and the planned time of execution.

Haman didn't set out to make an eleven-month gap, though. Rather, he relied on chance to inform and instruct him. We read in Esther 3:7, "In the first month, the month of Nisan, in King Ahasuerus's twelfth year, the Pur—that is, the lot—was cast before Haman for each day in each month, and it fell on the twelfth month, the month Adar." Lots were literally cast before Haman to determine the date of the destruction regarding the Jews.

As we've seen so far in our study on providence, there is no such thing as chance. The eleven-month gap that the casting of the lots provided was actually set up by God. He was the Puppet-Master behind the scenes arranging times, seasons, and events for His intended outcome. Bear in mind that whenever God creates a gap before any evil is about to occur, that gap is always good news in a bad situation.

Recall how God told Nineveh through Jonah that in forty days, Nineveh would be destroyed. Why didn't He just destroy them right then and there? Because He left open a window between judgment declared and judgment implemented. He left open a window of grace, where His mercy, movement, and miracles could still turn things around (Jonah 3:4). God gave the Jewish people a gap of eleven months to address the problem of Satanic influence in their enemies in order to seek to reverse their own destruction and continue His kingdom agenda on earth.

The Reason God Blesses You

Many of us know what it is like to have spiritual warfare waging against you so fiercely, continually, and thoroughly that all you can do is cry, similar to Mordecai. The pain gets so deep, the desperation feels so great that hopelessness becomes the only thought in our hearts and in our minds. This is exactly where Mordecai found himself when he heard that Haman's hatred stretched beyond him to his people. Esther 4:1 tells us, "When Mordecai learned all that had occurred, he tore his clothes, put on sackcloth and ashes, went into the middle of the city, and cried loudly and bitterly." Mordecai's panic and fear spread throughout the land as the letters traveled the pathways to the various pockets of people. In verse 3 we read, "There was great mourning among the Jewish people . . .

They fasted, wept, and lamented, and many lay in sackcloth and ashes."

While all of this was taking place, Esther was living behind the walls of the palace. She hadn't caught wind of the attack. In fact, as we will see later in the book of Esther, she hadn't even been speaking to the king for many days. But eventually Esther was told that Mordecai was in sackcloth and ashes, so she sent him clean clothes through a servant, offering her help. Esther's heart broke for Mordecai, so when he refused to change into the clothes she had sent, she asked one of her attendants to inquire as to why Mordecai was in mourning.

Mordecai's response came back straightforward and comprehensive. We read:

> Mordecai told him everything that had happened as well as the exact amount of money Haman had promised to pay the royal treasury for the slaughter of the Jews.
>
> Mordecai also gave him a copy of the written decree issued in Susa ordering their destruction, so that Hathach might show it to Esther, explain it to her, and command her to approach the king, implore his favor, and plead with him personally for her people. (Esther 4:7–8)

Essentially, Mordecai asked Esther's servant to take the actual edict to her and to tell her to go and let the king know who she was, and what ethnicity she was. Due to the anti-Semitic sentiments in the existing culture, Mordecai had previously advised Esther not to share about her bloodline. He knew that if she shared that information up front, she would be excluded from the options of women in line to be queen. But when the tables turned and the fate of an entire group of people had now been sealed by her husband's own signet ring, Mordecai altered his approach and asked Esther to come clean. He said it's now time to go public. It's now time to let it be known who she is and who her people happen to be. The time had come for Esther's true *season*.

You know that it is time for God to move you to your ultimate purpose when He gives you a position that enables you to leverage the influence He's given you for the advancement of His kingdom. This is exactly where Esther was. She had not been providentially chosen to be queen simply because she was pretty. Rather, God used the looks and temperament that He endowed her with in order to position her for influence and impact. God knew this day would come when a military strategy against His chosen people would be put into play. This is why He set Esther up specifically for this situation.

Friend, when God has positioned you to leverage your influence for kingdom purposes and the advancement of His agenda for His people, you are securely on the

> *God always blesses you to be a blessing.*

pathway to your destiny. God always blesses you to be a blessing. Not so the blessing will end with you, but so it will flow through you.

We have a terrible misunderstanding of what the definition and meaning of a blessing is in the day in which we live. So many believers are running around in life looking for their blessings. They are praying for their blessings. Calling on God in church for their blessings. But this is a flawed approach to God's blessings because it is an incomplete and unbiblical approach. Whenever you tell God that you want your blessing, period, that it is for you and to you and you alone, you have prostituted the term. This is because, biblically speaking, a blessing is only a blessing when it can flow through you and not just to you. In Genesis 12:2, God told Abraham, "I will make you a great nation, I will bless you, I will make your name great, and you will be a blessing."

Did you catch that last portion? It says, "And you will be a blessing." The reason for increasing and expanding Abraham's reach and impact through his family was to set him up so that through him God could deliver blessings to more people. God's goal is the advancement of His kingdom on earth, as well as the recognition of His glory. Whenever you go to God to ask Him for a blessing, always keep that in mind. Always include in your prayers or conversations with Him the ways in which His blessings to you can then be used as a blessing to others. Keep that mind-set as you go through each day, maximizing all that God has given to you in ways that will strengthen, bless, and help others. When God blesses you, He also has someone else in mind.

God doesn't just randomly choose to move you from a poorer part of town to a more established part of town for no reason. He doesn't have you trade in your bicycle for a Benz, just because. He doesn't enable you to shop elsewhere than the Salvation Army just so you can live large. He always has a reason for giving you more.

As with the life and story of Esther, He wants to know if you will use the pathway He has placed you on in ways that will advance His kingdom program. Will you use the gifts, talents, skills, and resources He has given you in an effort to bring Him glory and expand His kingdom domain on earth? Or will you simply use them for personal gain?

A gentle warning in this regard before we circle back to the situation Esther finds herself in. When there is little or no concern for God's kingdom in the use of the blessings He has given to you, you have literally just cut off your blessing. In fact, many people watch their blessings become a curse when they choose to hoard them for personal gain rather than kingdom expansion.

This was the dilemma set before Esther when she got the response from Mordecai. This was the decision she was up against. Was she to remain in her state of anonymity regarding her race and relative security, or would she step forward and declare who she was in an effort to help her people who were now doomed to annihilation?

Mordecai told Esther, in no uncertain terms, that it was time. It was time for her to use her position of influence, her resources, and her leverage in light of the spiritual battle at hand.

Esther responded to Mordecai, also in no uncertain terms, that what he was asking her to do was not practical. It was not strategic.

It was risky, foolish, and potentially life-threatening. In verse 11 of chapter 4 we read her reply:

> "All the royal officials and the people of the royal provinces know that one law applies to every man or woman who approaches the king in the inner courtyard and who has not been summoned—the death penalty—unless the king extends the gold scepter, allowing that person to live. I have not been summoned to appear before the king for the last thirty days." (Esther 4:11)

In my Tony Evans translation, she said:

"Mort, let me explain something. I need you to get this, cousin. It's sort of like this—see, me and the king have not been talking for thirty days now. We're not on good terms with each other. He hasn't invited me into his bed chamber. He's not talking to me so much anymore. In fact, it's been five years since he named me as his queen, and I've got a feeling he's not all that impressed with me much anymore. And see, we've got this simple rule in our house. If I go in and see him uninvited . . . and he doesn't hold out the royal scepter, well—it's over for me. And by over, I don't just mean I lose the crown. I mean I lose my head that holds the crown. They will put me to death. So what you are asking me to do, Mort, isn't that easy. You're asking me to risk my career, my economic stability, my palace—and what's more—my very life, all of it—for you, and the Jews."

Esther was at first unwilling to risk giving up favor with man in order to gain favor with God. She had become far too special for that in her own mind. She had stopped associating directly with the plight of her people, the Jews. She no longer lived like them in their shabby houses, eking out a life on a minimum wage. She no longer had to catch the bus, so to speak—or choose between just two changes of clothing. She no longer labored under the oppression of inferior living quarters and an inferior education offering inferior opportunities. No, she wasn't like those Jews. She used to be like them, but life was different now. Esther was an upper-class Jew now who no longer openly associated with her own people. She had become a successful Jew with a bank account, a chariot, and servants.

Thus, in her new socioeconomic, political scenario, she basically offered to feel sorry for them—the Jews—in hopes it would all work out for them. But to ask her to go and do something that could ultimately put her own life at risk, well—that was out of the question. That was just too much to ask of her right now.

And while that may appear to be a self-serving, cowardly decision of hers, before we judge Esther too quickly, isn't it similar to what many of us do now? We misdiagnose kingdom opportunity because we simply can't see it for what it is. We place personal preservation ahead of kingdom expansion, all in the name of security.

Yet what we are doing is also what Esther did when we refuse to take risks for God's agenda. We are forgetting that if it wasn't for the goodness of God in the first place, we wouldn't be where we are.

See, Esther had missed that reality in her assessment. She misunderstood that if it weren't for God's power and providence, she wouldn't be in the position she was in. She did not get there on her own. She got there the same way a turtle gets to the top of a fence—somebody put it there.

But it's easy to forget that, isn't it, when times are in our favor? It's easy to start thinking that life is all about me now. It's easy to hold back on risk and sacrifice because when things get comfortable, we have a natural tendency to preserve what we have for ourselves. It's easy to forget how you got where you are. Once you start living in a certain neighborhood, driving a certain vehicle, wearing certain clothes, and being degreed with certain degrees, it's easy to forget that if it weren't for the grace of God, you would not be in the position you are in.

And when you do forget that, like Esther did, you lose concern of how other people are going to get by in life. You wind up saying, in essence, "I made it—why aren't you making it too?" You become self-absorbed, which is the opposite of the atmosphere in God's kingdom, that of humility and service.

Friend, I want to let you in on some personal context as to why I feel so passionate about this. See, I'm not supposed to be where I am right now. I am not supposed to have reached this level of prominence and influence with my life. No, according to statistics,

I should be barely getting by. I was raised by parents who were not Christians until I was twelve years old. I was raised in a row housing section of urban Baltimore, where I was the first one in my family to graduate from high school. But because God invaded my home and led my father to Christ, changing my father's life, he wound up taking us to a Bible-teaching church. These changes also allowed me to have unique insights and opportunities, which then led to open doors. It is because of this history that I am where I am today. But I understand clearly that the only reason I am where I am today is because of the goodness and grace of God. And the moment I lose sight of that, my role has been illegitimatized.

God did not allow me the experiences and opportunities He has allowed me just so I could enjoy them. It's not only about me. It's about what God desires to do in and through me to advance His kingdom. Anybody who thinks otherwise will one day be held in account for having squandered the opportunities for service that the Lord gave them.

Your life—my life—Esther's life—all of our lives are about the kingdom of God. When we lose sight of that, we've missed God's plan and program in history. As Deuteronomy 8:18 states, "But remember that the LORD your God gives you the power to gain wealth, in order to confirm his covenant he swore to your fathers, as it is today."

God gives power. God makes wealth. God providentially sets you on the pathway of success for a kingdom purpose. It's okay to benefit from a kingdom purpose in your own personal life as long as you don't lose the focus of the kingdom purpose along the way. Because when you lose the kingdom purpose during the process of benefitting from the kingdom blessing, you likewise lose the fulfillment of your destiny.

The ultimate manifestation of your purpose will always involve a test, or multiple tests, to reach it. Like Pilgrim on the pathway to his intended destination in the famed classic book *Pilgrim's Progress*, you will face various trials and temptations appealing to the entire gamut of your emotions and weaknesses. How you respond to these will impact how quickly you reach your destiny.

Our responses and choices carry consequences in our lives, and because they do, we need people like Mordecai around us to speak the hard truth to us when we don't naturally respond as we should. We'll discover more about this as we turn the pages in this saga of the life of a woman named Esther.

CHAPTER FIVE

For Such a Time as This

 Your destiny will always involve a test. That test will always be aimed at whether you want to be a blessing or whether you merely want to be blessed. Because once you reach that test, God uses it to examine your heart.

Are you here for Him?

Are you here for how He can use you for others?

Or is this only about you?

If it's only about you, that's selfishness and self-preservation. That's removing yourself from God's covenantal covering of favor as you seek to grab as many treasures as you can stuff in your pockets. Doing so, like the fictional character in Aladdin, runs the risk of having you swallowed by the sands of personal gain.

Your value in the kingdom of God is found not in how much good you can get from God, but to what extent you let Him use you for the good of others.

Speaking of sand, sand on a beach is free. You can walk out onto any beach and pick up a handful of sand for free. Pick up as much as you want—sit in it, rub it all around. It's free. But that same sand, if you want to put it on a playground, is going to cost you something. You've got to go to the store now and buy bags of it in order to cover the surface of the playground. Why? Because it is being used differently. It's no longer free.

Now, if you want sandpaper to work on a project, that's going to cost you something as well. It's still sand, yes. It's sand glued onto paper. But you've got to go to a fix-it-up store and pay for a very small amount of this sand. While it's essentially the same free sand, it now has a higher value placed on it due to what its intended use will be and how it has been configured.

When you head into Silicon Valley where people are busy making computer chips with sand, you'll find an even higher price associated with sand. That's the most expensive sand you or I will come across. Not because it's different, but rather because it is used differently.

One of the reasons why God often doesn't do much with His people is that they aren't willing to be used by Him. They're just free sand with no purpose, intention, focus, or skill. They are just hanging out somewhere. What God is looking for is Silicon Valley Saints—saints who have learned that their value is tied to the extent of their usefulness in His kingdom. What good is a refrigerator that doesn't keep food cold? Or a stove that won't heat up food?

I recently had a single-service coffee maker in the kitchen that stopped working. It would make all of the sounds like it should when a cup of coffee was being brewed. It would light up like it should when a cup of coffee was being brewed. But no matter how long I stood there waiting for the cup of coffee to be poured out, nothing came out at all. You can imagine where this coffee maker wound up (and, no, it wasn't on the kitchen counter anymore).

The coffee maker's usefulness determined where and how it was positioned. Likewise, your usefulness to the Lord and His agenda determines the providential pathway He leads you on. Will you take the goodies and run? Or will you, like a wise businessperson, reinvest the assets of blessings He gives you in order to build a greater opportunity for growth, influence, and impact than ever before?

In Luke 14, God tells us how He feels about useless saints. In using salt as a comparison, Jesus explains:

> "Now, salt is good, but if salt should lose its taste, how will it be made salty? It isn't fit for the soil or for the manure pile; they throw it out. Let anyone who has ears to hear listen." (Luke 14:34–35)

Like my coffee maker that could no longer make coffee, saltless salt is "thrown out." A kingdom orientation must accompany and inform all that you do or you, too, will become useless for the kingdom.

God established His domain in such a way that His agenda exists to bring Him glory and expand His rule. We have each been called to the kingdom for such a purpose as this. When we shy away from this purpose out of selfishness, greed, or apathy, we cause ourselves to be useless for His kingdom.

Does that mean everyone should become a pastor? No, of course not. The kingdom of God involves the visible manifestation of His comprehensive rule over *every* area of life. There is not one single segment of society that excludes God's rule. What it means to be kingdom-oriented is to intentionally pursue His purposes on the providential pathways within the realm of influence where He has placed you.

A kingdom orientation must accompany and inform all that you do.

Living Mannequins

My good friend Tony Dungy, the famed former coach for the Indianapolis Colts, used to call me every week during the year he won the Super Bowl. Each week we would talk on the phone about a variety of subjects. We'd always end in prayer. Once Coach Dungy made it to the playoffs, his prayer became focused on this new venture. When I would ask him what he'd like for me to pray with him about, he would inevitably reply, "My prayer is simple, Tony—that win or lose, I will make His name great before this expanded national audience."

Once Coach Dungy made it into the Super Bowl game and his team was slated to face the Chicago Bears, I thought that his prayer might change—not much, but some—toward winning. Yet when I went to ask Coach what he wanted me to pray for, he simply said, "Tony, the world is watching. Win or lose, I want to make it inextricably clear that I belong to Jesus Christ. I do not want to miss this moment as a witness for Him." What's my point in sharing this story with you? Coach Dungy had made a kingdom connection to coaching football.

Kingdom, and God's agenda, correlates with everything He has given us to do. Nothing sits outside of His direct rule and intended purposes for it to bring Him glory and expand the reach of His name.

Large, high-end department stores will often have over-sized display windows that face the street. These windows are often filled with dummies, also known as mannequins. The mannequins are clothed in the most current trends and positioned in such a way so as to draw the attention of the passers-by on the street. Some of the very expensive stores will even go to great lengths in employing living mannequins to stand in their windows, clothed in their fashions, in an effort to attract people into their stores. One time when my wife, Lois, and I were walking in New York City, we literally saw a living mannequin sitting in a Ferrari in a display window!

Why do the owners of these department stores go to such efforts in filling the windows with such elaborate displays? The reason they do this is so that when people are walking down the street, they will be impressed by what they see and that will then draw them into the store to shop. These dressed-up dummies draw potential customers into a kingdom of clothes and merchandise that has floor after floor after floor of so much more.

Friend, when God blesses you, He does so with the intention of putting you on display. He allows you to be successful, obtain your education, have the resources that you do, gain popularity or notoriety, so that you will be seen as a representative of His kingdom who has been touched by the favor and grace of God Himself. But don't go and get the big head when He clothes you in such fine designer threads. Because if you start to think *you* got yourself to where you are now, you will forget that it was His providential leading and provision which made you into what you are today.

We must all remember that on our best day, we are sinners saved by grace.

The sinking of the *Titanic* was a terrible accident that happened over a hundred years ago. But what makes the situation all the more tragic is that the deaths that occurred did not have to occur. Most of the lifeboats coming off of the *Titanic* as she went down were only half-filled. But since the people in the lifeboats were already delivered and they didn't want to risk turning back to help others, many people died that day who didn't have to.

God did not save you to sit, soak, and sour. He has not left you or me here just to make it until we get to glory. He has left us on earth because there are a lot of people drowning all around us—they are drowning spiritually, relationally, emotionally, morally, financially, and more. But far too many of us share the sentiments of Esther in her initial response to Mordecai. We're content to remain in our own secure lifeboat, making it all about us.

But you do not exist just for yourself. You exist to make a difference—an impact.

For example, bowlers are known by their impact. It doesn't matter how good-looking a bowler is, or how fancy his or her outfit is, or even how shiny the ball is. These days there are stylish bowling socks, bags, balls, and all else. But no matter what a bowler has to make him look good, the real testament to the bowler comes by seeing how many pins are still standing after he rolls the ball. It's *impact* that establishes the value of the bowler, and nothing else.

> *You do not exist just for yourself.*

Similarly, it matters not how Christian-y you appear to be, or how churchified you come across with all of your paraphernalia or "Christianese." If there is no impact for the kingdom of God through your life, then you have failed as a representative of the King. Until God sees that He can use you to accomplish His goals, He is not going to open up the providential pathways to the purpose He has for you to fulfill. Why would He do so if you are merely going to dismiss it and wander elsewhere? No, you and I are blessed to be a blessing.

Like Esther.

Back to Esther

Esther just didn't know that at first. It took a stern reminder from her cousin to wake her up and speak some sense into her life. In one of the most well-known passages of Scripture, we find a rebuke from a relative who knew his loved one had somehow gotten off track. Mordecai sent back this firm message to Esther:

> "Don't think that you will escape the fate of all the Jews because you are in the king's palace. If you keep silent at this time, relief and deliverance will come to the Jewish people from another place, but you and your father's family will be destroyed. Who knows, perhaps you have come to your royal position for such a time as this." (Esther 4:13–14)

I can hear my favorite R&B group, The Temptations, singing in the background now, "It's just your imagination . . . running away with you!" Mordecai urged Esther to not allow her imagination to run away with her, tricking her into believing that she was safe from the edict simply because she lived in the palace. He showed her that she was somehow caught under the mistaken idea that by not risking her life in approaching the king she was somehow saving it. Her life had already been marked. She was a

Jew. So Mordecai set about to shape her theology by informing her that if she didn't rise to this occasion by mustering the courage to approach the king, God would raise up a solution through someone else. No one, not even Esther, is indispensable. If God can create the universe out of nothing, He doesn't need any of us to accomplish His designed will.

I'll write this as gently as I can, but truth be told, it doesn't matter how good you are, how rich you are, how powerful you are, or even how skilled you are. God never limits Himself to one person. God always has something up His sleeve. He doesn't reveal it until He needs to do so, but God always has hidden options. He always has an alternate route, another pathway to accomplishing His purpose.

> *God always has something up His sleeve.*

I live in Dallas, and if I were to drive to downtown Dallas, I'd take the main highway. It's called Interstate 35. But what most people don't know who are not from here is that if traffic ever looks bad on Interstate 35, there are other ways to get downtown. For one, I can get off at Illinois and then head on over to Zang. I can also go through South Dallas via Fair Park. There is more than one pathway to reach the destination. Similarly, God has more than one person and method to bring about His will.

What Mordecai wanted Esther to remember was that while God would prefer to use her in the king's palace, and while God had positioned her to be used in her role and status, through her beauty and character, He could also easily find someone else. God is never, ever boxed into a corner. He always keeps His options open when it comes to carrying out His promises.

One of the most dangerous things we can do as disciples of the King is think too highly of ourselves. When it comes down to it, neither you—nor I—are "all that." Yes, God may have chosen to bless us, position us, or bring us to a place of influence, but that's because He wants to use us. And the moment He discovers you are unwilling to be used for His kingdom purposes, He can just as easily raise up someone else to replace you.

Disobedience to your kingdom calling runs the risk of losing your kingdom calling. Wandering off the pathway of purpose runs the risk of wandering in the wilderness of waste. God will never force you to fulfill your destiny. God will enable you to live out your purpose, but it's up to you, through your choices and character, to remain in it.

Success is often the greatest deterrent to future success. Whether it's in business, sports, or personal relationships, once humanity tastes victory it causes a number of things to happen. Enlarged egos often reduce drive and dependence on God, for one. Pride swallows humility, for another. Power can corrupt. It can also give birth to complacency. Knowing this, Mordecai had to make his point to Esther as plain as day. In seeking to save the success she'd attained up to that point, she was actually putting herself at the greatest risk of losing it. Was entering the king's palace uninvited her largest concern? Was that action truly the one action that would put her life at risk? In her mind, it was. But in God's economy, not doing so was even riskier. God had called Esther for this specific season and this specific need. If she chose to seek security over obedience, she could lose it all.

If You Remain Silent

Many people quote this rebuke by Mordecai as a life-verse denoting prestige, power, and favor. You'll see shirts, hats, mugs, and social media posts that proudly ring out, "for such a time as this." But few people truly connect the context of the verse with how they are using it. Esther was being chided for her self-indulgent, self-preserving mind-set. Esther was being reproofed for living large and embracing royalty over service. Through those telling words, Mordecai was reminding Esther that she had been chosen to set her own interests aside, let go of her own ambitions, and face an enemy full-on. She had been called to wield her influence, cunningly strategize her decisions, and seek to overturn a dynasty bent on destruction.

> *Mordecai was reminding Esther that she had been chosen to set her own interests aside, let go of her own ambitions, and face an enemy full-on.*

If you're a superhero fan, Esther can be compared to Wonder Woman. She had been called into a fierce battle as a woman warrior.

She had to be willing to get dirty, take a hit, and defend an entire people dependent upon her. She was to risk her life and her legacy with no guarantees of a positive outcome.

That's the "for such a time as this" Esther was challenged to accept.

And that's the "for such a time as this" God also sets before you.

It is God who has given you your job, position, resources, education, and more. Whether male or female, it is God who has opened the opportunities for you to optimize for His kingdom purposes. He didn't place you where you are so you could eat figs all day long. He's placed you where you are because you are in the midst of a battle, a war. You are in the midst of a seismic conflict involving Good versus Evil. You are in the midst of a feud for the spoils of lost souls. You are in your own Bird vs. Goliath conflict, representing the Holy Spirit within you (Luke 3:22).

To miss your kingdom assignment because you have become too caught up in your personal kingdom is the greatest tragedy you could ever face. To exist in life without carrying out the accomplishment of why you were put here in the first place is to squander the gifts, skills, and blessings you've received so far. If your life isn't focused on winning people to Christ, discipling them in the faith, and improving their lives in history so that they, too, can be greater vessels for God's kingdom, then Mordecai's words are directed to you as well. Go ahead and insert your name where the pronoun *you* appears:

"If *you* keep silent at this time, relief and deliverance will come . . . from another place, but *you* and *your* father's family will be destroyed."

You have been called to demonstrate the power of the kingdom of heaven in history. You have been created to live as a kingdom disciple, heaven's representative on earth. Attending church is not your purpose. If that's the entirety of your spiritual life, you have merely added a weekly gathering to your social calendar in the name of Jesus. No, God put you on earth for much more than that.

You have been called to the kingdom for such a time as this.

For such a time in our culture where decay has taken root.

For such a time in our families where millions of young people exist without so much as a mentor to help steer their way.

For such a time in our communities where the lost go without hope and the hurt go without healing.

For such a time in our world where people die for lack of clean water, lives get derailed for lack of direction, and an entire generation questions the faith for lack of authentic disciples leading the way.

The kingdom is bigger than the church. The kingdom is bigger than your small group Bible study. These things are good. These things are necessary. But they exist to facilitate the advancement of God's kingdom; they are not the kingdom itself.

If I Perish

Mordecai's rebuke shook Esther, reminding her of the reality she lived in rather than the façade she had come to believe was real. Her response indicated that she "got it." She understood what he was saying. We read:

> "Go and assemble all the Jews who can be found in Susa and fast for me. Don't eat or drink for three days, night or day. I and my female servants will also fast in the same way. After that, I will go to the king even if it is against the law. If I perish, I perish." (Esther 4:16)

Let me tell you another way you will know it's your time and your season. There will be a spiritual conflict that God asks you to intervene in. You will see how He has prepared you to be a blessing and not just to be blessed. But then He will ask you to take a risk of faith. While Esther realized God could use someone else besides her if she chose not to step out in faith, she also realized to step out in faith was risky too. That's why she ended her reply to Mordecai with, "If I perish, I perish."

Faith is risky business. It's risky because you are dealing with something you cannot see. The opposite of faith is sight. If you can see it, it's not faith. If you can know the outcome, it's not faith. If you can see the destination during every turn and twist on the pathway, it's not faith. Following a GPS that outlines the entire path you are driving clear to the arrival point is not faith. Faith, however, is acting on what you do not see. Faith is taking one step when it's only one step you see simply because you believe God wants you to do it based on His Word. It is taking a step without being assured of the destination.

Most of us don't mind taking a step when we can guarantee the outcome. But risky faith isn't based on that. Esther-faith isn't based on that. The greater the uncertainty, the greater the faith and dependency on God. The more looming the potential danger or risk, the more powerful the purpose. The more fearful the step, the more full the faith. Sometimes God calls us to take a step when we cannot see where our foot is going to land. Esther didn't know if the king would hold out his scepter. But because she knew she'd been given a unique, royal opportunity for such a time as this to save her people from certain death, she chose to take that step of faith.

> *The more looming the potential danger or risk, the more powerful the purpose.*

All through the Bible, people had to take risky steps of faith whenever God wanted to do something big through them. It's spiritual entrepreneurialism to take these risks, based on God's Word and His leading, in order to invest in a greater spiritual future than what you have right then. Esther was a strategic spiritual entrepreneur. She knew what she was up against. That's why she asked everyone to fast for three days and three nights. If she was going to risk her well-being on their behalf, she needed them invested as well. No war is ever won by one foot soldier. Esther was wise enough to realize this and seek spiritual support. She knew she needed to go before the heavenly King prior to approaching the earthly king.

The challenge to you through the story of Esther involves this: open your eyes to recognize that you have been called to the kingdom for such a time as this. A turtle only makes progress when it sticks its neck out. God wants to use you. God wants to bless you. God wants to empower you. But He is testing you to see if you are willing to stick with Him and His kingdom agenda when the going gets tough. Or, if you will simply duck and run for cover.

Our nation, communities, families, and friends need each of us to live at a higher kingdom level. With so much destruction occurring all around us, and even in us, we need to step out into the uncertainty of faith while following the certainty of the One who calls us. We need to proclaim boldly to our King:

"Use me in whatever way You choose. Even in uncertainty, I'll take the risk. Just show me what You want me to do. Show me why You have placed me here and how You are guiding me."

Then, when He shows you, be willing to do what He says. No matter the cost. No matter the potential for loss. No matter the risk. You have been called to the kingdom for a purpose much greater than your own personal pleasure and gain. You have been called to the kingdom of God for such a time as this.

CHAPTER SIX

Guess Who's Coming to Dinner

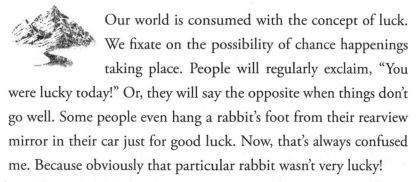 Our world is consumed with the concept of luck. We fixate on the possibility of chance happenings taking place. People will regularly exclaim, "You were lucky today!" Or, they will say the opposite when things don't go well. Some people even hang a rabbit's foot from their rearview mirror in their car just for good luck. Now, that's always confused me. Because obviously that particular rabbit wasn't very lucky!

The book of Esther, on the other hand, drives one point home over and over again. That point is that there is no such thing as luck. Rather, it is providence. Sure, providence looks like luck, feels like luck—it may even smell like luck. Providence gives the impression of chance happenings at hand. But the reality is that the

Puppet-Master is always at work behind the scenes, maneuvering and matching for His intended outcomes. God takes the good, the bad, and the ugly and makes it look like it just happened randomly. He either causes, or allows, things and events to happen which will ultimately usher in His will.

Providence is God's way of staying anonymous. In those times when He doesn't want to be out front as the great, spectacular God, He will work behind the scenes, providentially tweaking, twisting, and setting things up. In these occasions, scenarios seem like coincidences. But in God's kingdom, a coincidence is simply one of those times when He chooses not to make His presence known. God is the author and maker of coincidences. He is the intentional heart behind what appears to be random happenings. He is the orchestrator of events and the delegator of roles. It is He who strategically placed Esther in the status as queen so that when the time came for His chosen people to face yet another aggressive, hate-filled enemy, Esther would be positioned to intervene.

Game Time

As we saw in the last chapter, Esther had requested that her people fast with her for three days before going to the king. On the third day of the fast, Esther put on her royal robe and entered the inner court of the king. This is the moment of decision. This is game time. This is the time that will tell all. Is the king going to extend to her his favor, or has she seen the last of her days?

I can imagine that Esther's heart pounded within her as she stepped quietly into the inner court. Her knees may have felt weak beneath the weight of her worry. Was her gaze down, in submission? Or did she seek to portray an aura of confidence, as if she should be there all along? Scripture doesn't go into details of Esther's entrance but it does tell us the king's response. Esther 5:2 says, "As soon as the king saw Queen Esther standing in the courtyard, she gained favor in his eyes. The king extended the gold scepter in his hand toward Esther, and she approached and touched the tip of the scepter."

She could breathe. At least a bit. The king had responded to her in favor, and indicated a willingness to have her in his presence. In fact, his next statement reveals more than just a willingness to have her in his presence. It reveals a sentiment toward her of kindness and trust. Asking why she had come to see him, the king went on to say, "What is troubling you, Queen Esther? And what is your request? Even to half of the kingdom it shall be given to you" (v. 3 NASB).

The king pulled what I call a "kingdom man" move right there. He stuck three fingers in the air, in my Tony Evans translation, and said, "Esther, I got it." Whatever was wrong, whatever was disturbing her—the king was going to fix it. Three fingers up in the air means "he's got it."

From a Fast to a Feast

We get a peek into Esther's wisdom and character in her response. Rather than blurt out what's bothering her or demand that her husband do something to turn it around, Esther believed that her next best move would be to invite the king to dinner, along with the enemy of her people—Haman. It's been said that the way to a man's heart is through his stomach. Esther seemed to know this as well. Instead of going straight for the heart of the matter concerning her, Esther went straight for delighting the taste buds of her king. In response to his question, she told him that a special banquet had been prepared for them to feast at. I'm sure this banquet had all of the king's favorite dishes, as well as his favorite drinks. Keep in mind, banquets in the day and age of Esther didn't just get popped into the oven or microwave to heat up. Even if it was only for a few people to dine, each dish had to be well-planned out and prepared in advance. Thus, while the Jews and Esther had set about fasting for three days, Esther was simultaneously planning a feast. It's never wise to grocery shop on an empty stomach because you wind up buying too much, but it may have been wise in her case. No doubt the meal had been carefully prepped and plated with the utmost of attention to both flavor and detail.

Before we go any deeper into Esther's narrative, let me explain an important spiritual principle that she exemplifies through this foresight on her part. The principle is this: You will never get to see God's providence at work in your circumstances until and unless God sees you move in accordance with His will. The reason Esther fasted and prayed and asked others to join her in fasting and praying was because she needed insight into how to approach this dangerous situation. She needed divine insight into a difficult problem. Yet even *while* she was fasting and praying, she was working. Esther wasn't sitting around doing nothing. The banquet she invited the king and Haman to attend was already prepared by the time she had invited them. The menu had already been chosen. The banquet was served on the very day she entered his inner court. In verse 4 we read this clearly: "'If it pleases the king,' Esther replied, 'may the king and Haman come today to the banquet I have prepared for them.'" "Have prepared" is past tense. Esther did more than fast and pray; she followed God's leading in movement along the way.

> *You will never get to see God's providence at work in your circumstances until and unless God sees you move in accordance with His will.*

Thus, her invitation to the king is an invitation couched in confident faith. It demonstrates an assumption that the king is going to accept it. The food has already been made, and is ready to be served. Esther didn't live in the time of TV dinners. A banquet required some planning to create. Thus, while Esther entered into a time of fasting—an intentional decision to give up the craving of the physical because of a greater need in the spiritual—she also entered into a time of planning. As she heard from God during her time with and before Him, she responded to His leading.

One of the reasons we miss the so-called "coincidences" of God in our lives is that we do not have a raised antenna toward Him. We do not set aside cravings of the flesh for answers in the spiritual. What's more, when we fail to pick up spiritual signals and directions, we cannot act on them. So we wind up operating according to our human viewpoint and our natural perspective.

What fasting and prayer does is lift our antenna toward the spiritual realm to pick up the picture from heaven that we need to see in order to know what to do on earth. The first thing Esther did once she committed to moving forward in a difficult situation was to admit that she needed God. She needed to talk to and hear from God because she didn't know how to overcome this obstacle ahead of her. One wrong move could cost her a career, her finances, her home, and even her life. So not only did Esther talk to God but she gathered everyone who would to talk to Him on her behalf as well.

Steps of Faith

Another critical spiritual principle that we glean from Esther's dinner invitation to the king is that she didn't rely on past victories and past strategies for present situations. If you recall in the earlier part of her narrative, Esther had chosen to take very little into the king on the night she was chosen to spend with him. She had decided not to go all out and create a fancy evening full of trinkets and charms, but rather relied on the simplicity of her own sincere spirit to cultivate trust. Yet in this case, as she sought the Lord and His leading, Esther threw everything into the equation—including the kitchen sink. She set about planning an elaborate banquet fit for a king—a king who knew well how to party and dine. Remember, this is the same king who had once thrown a party that lasted six entire months. His party standards were high. Yet, Esther was up for the challenge. Because when all was in place, Esther did the next thing the Lord asks of each of us to do when faced with challenges too big to overcome on our own. She took a step of faith. She walked into the king's inner court to offer her invitation.

Far too many of us are waiting on God to move when God is really waiting on us. As you read and study through the Scriptures, you'll see a pattern regularly occur. Most of the time when God was getting ready to do something big for someone or for a group of people, He cleared the path for the people to do something. The people had to move in faith, even when they could not see what God was doing. Moses had to hold out the rod and the people had to move before God would open up the Red Sea (Exod. 14:21). The priests had to step into the river before God would open up the Jordan River (Josh. 3:14–16). Martha and the others had to move the stone before God would raise up Lazarus from the dead (John 11:41–44). Time and time again, God would not move until the people moved in faith.

God is testing whether you actually believe Him, or just say you believe Him.

Faith is measured by footsteps. It's measured by your feet. Faith shows up in your walk, not only in your talk. It manifests through your life, not just through your lips. Faith makes itself known through your movements, not just your mouth.

When there are no footsteps to back up your faith, it's not faith. You can't sit at home and ask God to give you a job while not going job-hunting. Have you ever seen a bird sitting on a branch with its beak open just waiting for worms to drop in from heaven? Neither have I. While birds expect God to provide them with their food for sustenance, they also know they have to go hunting to get it. God must see faith in action because "without faith it is impossible to please God" (Heb. 11:6). Faith is measured by what you do, not just by what you talk about doing.

After Esther fasted for three days, and after the preparations for the banquet had been made, she took another step of faith. Then the next step. And then the next. All the way up to the golden scepter. What did Esther get in return? Well, so far she got the open door to the next step of faith to take. This step involved the plan of inviting her husband to dinner, along with the enemy Haman. In this way, Esther got Haman on home-court advantage. She moved Haman into her territory.

What fasting and prayer did for Esther was allow God to reveal to her a plan. When she didn't know what to do, God gave her an idea. He had to plant a thought in her mind about something that wouldn't naturally come up on her own. This is because God knows the end from the beginning. As you see Esther's story play out, you'll come to realize just how strategic this dinner turned out to be. But Esther wouldn't know that ahead of time. Because Esther is like us—we can only see what we see in the present and in the past. What connecting with God in the spiritual realm provides is the opportunity to tap into an approach that goes beyond the natural and into the heart of providence.

Take, for instance, Daniel. Daniel is another biblical character whose approach to a dilemma rested on his relationship with the Lord. When we come across Daniel in chapter 1 of the book by his name, we find him having been taken into another pagan city by another king—Nebuchadnezzar. Nebuchadnezzar had set about a system wherein he sought to deprogram the young Israelite boys from their culture, faith, and heritage, while simultaneously reprogramming them into a purely Babylonian worldview. Part of that worldview involved food. Yet when ordered to eat the meat that had been sacrificed to idols, Daniel refused to do so (Dan. 1:8). He could not violate God's command in order to obey the king. Having told his overseer about his decision, the overseer pushed back—with good reason. After all, if he was unable to have Daniel and his friends eat the meat according to the king's command, then it would be his own life taken for punishment (Dan. 1:10). The overseer wasn't seeking to be argumentative for argument's sake. He was in a chain of command that required obedience, or else.

Yet after Daniel stepped forward to announce his decision of risky faith, because of his belief in God, God stepped in. And guess what God gave to Daniel. No, it wasn't an army of angels to annihilate the Babylonians. Nor was it the muscle-power of Samson to overpower them by himself. Rather, God gave Daniel an idea.

He placed a strategy within his mind that would enable him to maneuver toward his intended goal. Daniel said, "Please test your servants for ten days. Let us be given some vegetables to eat and water to drink. Then examine our appearance and the appearance of the young men who are eating the king's food, and deal with your servants based on what you see" (Dan. 1:12–13).

God had given Daniel an approach that would work. After the ten days, the overseer saw that Daniel and his friends were more vibrant, strong, and healthy than the others, so they were allowed to continue in their obedience to their kingdom values.

But keep in mind that God didn't give Daniel the idea until he had stepped out in faith. Many of us are waiting for God to show up and do something in our lives, but at the same time, God is waiting until we show up and step out in faith.

God didn't show up for the three Hebrew boys who were tossed in the fiery furnace until after they had taken their stand for God (Dan. 3). He didn't show up for Daniel, once again, until Daniel continued in prayer against the king's command and was thus tossed into the lions' den (Dan. 6). The Bible is replete with examples like this.

The reason why so many of us are not seeing God maneuver and intersect things for us in our favor, even though we may be trying to manipulate them ourselves, is because we are not moving as He wants us to move. We are not employing faith in action based on what we do know. As a result, there are no ideas coming into our minds on how to deal with the impossible situations we are facing.

Parties, Patience, and Providence

Esther's people are set to be annihilated. Her own ethnicity is a secret. So she throws the king a banquet. She hosts a party! I'm fairly certain that specific military strategy would have never shown up in anyone's minds on their own. But God's ways are not our ways, which is why we must humble ourselves in dependence upon Him to tap into the wisdom of His providential path.

It's a good thing Esther was prepared with the banquet, because the king didn't hesitate when he got her invitation. We read in Esther 5:5–6 that the king pretty much dropped what he was doing and went to her banquet. It says:

> The king said, "Hurry, and get Haman so we can do as Esther has requested." So the king and Haman went to the banquet Esther had prepared.
>
> While drinking the wine, the king asked Esther, "Whatever you ask will be given to you. Whatever you want, even to half the kingdom, will be done."

After the food and following the wine, the offer still stood. Up to "half of the kingdom" the king put his pledge before her once again. But Esther wasn't biting. While common sense might say, "Take it—he's just offered you all you need," Esther paused. God didn't give her the freedom to move forward. So what did she do instead? She replied respectfully:

"This is my petition and my request: If I have found favor in the eyes of the king, and if it pleases the king to grant my petition and perform my request, may the king and Haman come to the banquet I will prepare for them. Tomorrow I will do what the king has asked." (Esther 5:7–8)

Say what? The man just told her that he's going to give her half of the kingdom. What else could she want? After all, she had made this dinner in order to request that he save her people from the genocide stemming from Haman's hate. She had both men sitting there, drinking wine and filling their stomachs. Everything looked to be ready, especially when the king willingly offered up to her, once again, up to half of his kingdom.

Yet rather than jump in and state her request, Esther once again stuck to the leading within. She stuck to the strategy God had placed in her mind. Rather than state her case, Esther asked them to come back to a banquet again. This banquet would be held the very next night. Now, keep in mind—Esther wasn't asking them to come back for leftovers. She had put a plan in place to invite the king and Haman for dinner, not knowing what God was going to do between Dinner One and Dinner Two. This is because obedience doesn't require full knowledge of how God is going to work things out. Obedience means doing what God has asked you to do while leaving the unknowns in His hands.

And two of these "unknowns" were about to make all the difference in the world.

CHAPTER SEVEN

That Night

 Following the first banquet, Haman left the king's palace feeling satisfied and smug. He had been invited to eat with the king and the queen. Not only that, he was the only guest who had been invited. Haman's heart swelled with pride, no doubt. Thus, when he ran across Mordecai on his way out, Mordecai's failure to bow before him once again filled him with even more hatred and rage than before.

He already disdains the man. He's already ticked off at him. But to insult him when he had just come from one of the highest personal honors in the land was more than Haman could stand. Haman then did what many men do when things get under their skin. He went home and told his friends and his wife. He vented. It's recorded that:

Then Haman described for them his glorious wealth and his many sons. He told them all how the king had honored him and promoted him in rank over the other officials and the royal staff. "What's more," Haman added, "Queen Esther invited no one but me to join the king at the banquet she had prepared. I am invited again tomorrow to join her with the king. Still, none of this satisfies me since I see Mordecai the Jew sitting at the King's Gate all the time." (Esther 5:11–13)

Haman stroked his own ego in the company of those who would agree, and then waited for their response about the one thing that still nagged him. Their response came quickly enough. They advised Haman to build gallows fifty cubits high first thing in the morning and then ask the king to have Mordecai hung on it. After which, they told him to go joyfully to the second banquet.

Haman's family and friends suggested a way to get rid of Mordecai because he was messing with him. He had made the best day of Haman's life miserable through his open display of disrespect. He deserved to die on those gallows, according to Haman's homeboys. And Haman agreed.

Which brings us to our next critical event that happened between the two banquets. This one involved the king. Chapter 6 of Esther starts off with these telling words, "*That* night sleep escaped the king . . ." (emphasis added). Note that the text is not referring to just any night. It specifically points out that what is about to be told happened "that night." This is not just an ordinary night. It is a special night because it is a night surrounding a special set of circumstances which involve a special set of people.

What night is this? It's the very night that the queen hosted the first dinner. It's the very night that Haman is thinking he's the boss. It's the very night that Haman comes home to his family and friends and tells how ticked off he is. It's also *that* very night that Haman sets in place a plan to build gallows upon which Mordecai will be killed the very next day.

It's *that* night. This is not just any old, regular night. This is a very particular night when a very particular thing occurs: The king cannot sleep.

Insomnia sets in.

The king tosses and turns every which way because something just so "happens" to be keeping him awake. Something just so "happens" to be keeping him unstable. Something just so "happens" to be keeping him off balance. Proverbs 21:1 gives us insight into that something where we read, "A king's heart is like channeled water in the Lord's hand: He directs it wherever he chooses." On *that* night, God directed it back and forth on top of his covers. He wouldn't let the king fall asleep.

Yes, God even knows how to keep people from sleeping when He needs to do so to accomplish His sovereign program and plan. Keep in mind, we aren't just reading about *a* night. No, we are reading about *that* night when heaven has to intervene in history or Mordecai will be killed and Esther's request for her people will most likely go unspoken. It's the night when the fingerprints of the

Puppet-Master are working out His plans by gently tugging on the king each time he nearly drifts off to sleep.

So what did the king do to help alleviate his sleeplessness? According to Esther 6:1, he told his servant to go get him something boring to read. While he doesn't say the word "boring" in what's recorded in Scripture, he does call for the reading of the records and chronicles which, to me, and to most of us, would be boring. All of those names, dates, places, and events were sure to do the trick. The king was tired. No doubt he was frustrated. To help himself get some rest, he ordered his servant to head down to the library and grab the records. When counting sheep no longer works, you can always try reading the historical chronicles. Why not?

The servant went and got the book and began reading to the king. Now, I can imagine that a book of chronicles recording the history and details of a nation's daily occurrences would have many, many pages. It was probably many, many inches thick. But bear in mind that it just so "happened" that the servant just so "happened" to flip right to the page that had to do with Mordecai. Some might call that a lucky flip. Others could call it chance. There are even those who might use the word "fate" to describe flipping through hundreds, if not thousands, of pages right to the one that matters most.

I call it providence. It's the Puppet-Master at work.

In the Chronicles, the servant read to the king how Mordecai had once reported a situation concerning two men who had been plotting to lay hands on him and kill him. They had been two of the king's eunuchs who served as door-keepers. As the servant reads, the once-sleepy king suddenly sits up in bed. I imagine it may have gone something like this:

"That man saved my life?" the king asks.

Startling into alertness, the servant replies, "Well, yes—he did."

"What's his name?" the king inquires.

"It says his name is Mordecai," the servant speaks clearly.

We pick up the conversation in the book of Esther where we read that the king then asks, "What honor or special recognition have been given to Mordecai for this act?" (Esther 6:3).

The servant replied that he was not aware of any honor or dignity being given to this man named Mordecai. "Nothing?" the king may have said, curious as to why.

"No, nothing," the servant would have affirmed.

Keep in mind, this is all happening on *that* night. That night where Esther lay wondering what she's going to do the next night at dinner. That night where an entire race of people remained locked in certain doom under an edict of annihilation. That night when Mordecai's life had been earmarked for hanging on the very next day. Yes, it's *that* night on which the king could not sleep and then asked for a book of records—any book of records—to be brought and read to him. It's *that* night when a man named Mordecai's heroic deed from days gone by is brought to the forefront of the king's mind.

The Web of Providence

Friend, God's providence is tied to time. The book of Esther covers years, even decades. We start out with her as a young girl in a period of time when Queen Vashti gets cast away. Then later Esther is chosen to enter a beauty contest of sorts where all the lovely women of the kingdom get a chance to marry the king. Now, as "luck" would have it—Esther gets chosen to be queen. More years pass by when we reach a point where Haman—a descendant of the Agagites and sworn enemies of the Jews—gets enraged by Esther's relative and sets out to have the Jews killed. Mordecai pleads with Esther to stand up for her people and she requests three days within which to pray, fast, and prepare. Then she throws a banquet for the king and Haman, only to have Haman become even angrier after he leaves, and put plans in place to kill Mordecai the very next day.

Providence weaves through time and circumstances like a spider carefully crafting its web. Each movement may not appear to be leading to anything significant until the entire web has been completed, but every movement and motion matters.

This is why you must trust God's heart even when you do not understand His hand.

Returning to the king on *that* night, we discover that while he's in the middle of discussing Mordecai and what had been done to honor him for saving his life, he heard some rustling just outside of his chambers. Wondering who was there, he inquired as to who it was. Early morning had come and an eager Haman had hastily made his way to ask for the king's permission to hang Mordecai. It's doubtful Haman had slept much that night either.

The story unfolds for us in Esther 6 where we read:

> The king asked, "Who is in the court?" Now Haman was just entering the outer court of the palace to ask the king to hang Mordecai on the gallows he had prepared for him.
>
> The king's attendants answered him, "Haman is there, standing in the court."
>
> "Have him enter," the king ordered. Haman entered, and the king asked him, "What should be done for the man the king wants to honor?" Haman thought to himself, "Who is it the king would want to honor more than me?" (vv. 4–6)

Keep in mind, we're still talking about *that* night. We're still in the same place in time. It's on the night that Haman gets ticked off so much so that he wants to kill Mordecai right then and there. The night that the king can't sleep. It's still that night that the king calls for someone to read him the book of records and they so happened to read the part where Mordecai saved his life. And it is early *that* morning—the very morning where the king is wondering just how to honor Mordecai—that Haman reenters the picture with a question of his own. But before Haman can get to his question, the king starts in on his, "What should be done for the man the king wants to honor?"

Now, Haman assumes the king is talking about him. Haman thinks the king is thinking of his number-two man. Haman feels like he's walked into yet another opportunity to elevate himself. So Haman answers the king with an elaborate description of what should be done when the king wants to show honor. After all, how often does a king ask a question like that? The next few verses give us insight into Haman's mind-set, as well as his detailed reply:

> Haman thought to himself, "Who is it the king would want to honor more than me?" Haman told the king, "For the man the king wants to honor: Have them bring a royal garment that the king himself has worn and a horse the king himself has ridden, which has a royal crown on its head. Put the garment and the horse under the charge of one of the king's most noble officials. Have them clothe the man the king wants to honor, parade him on the horse through the city square, and proclaim before him, 'This is what is done for the man the king wants to honor.'" (Esther 6:6b–9)

Haman was more than happy to help out the king in setting up what needed to be done to honor whom he thought was himself. Now, you have to understand that when a person would put on the king's robe and ride the king's horse and be paraded across the square as a representative of the king—it's telling everyone in the domain that the person being shown this honor is the king-in-waiting. He is the master behind the scenes. Everyone else is just an understudy. Haman spared no spoils in concocting the most emphatic, statement-making method for the king to show honor to him.

There was just one small, ironic problem. It actually only came down to one word. Had one additional word been added to the king's conversation with Haman, it would have changed everything Haman had said. Everything. And that word was, "Mordecai." All the king would have had to have said differently is, "What should I do for Mordecai to honor him?" and all plans Haman just offered up would be off the table. No horse. No robe. No public proclamation of honor. He'd probably offer up some chicken and waffles, or suggest that they take him shopping—and all the while he would be seething underneath. Yet since Haman assumed the king had been talking about him, his answer involved a lot more than a run through the drive-through at Church's Fried Chicken. Leaving out one word changed the trajectory of the whole conversation.

It changed everything until the king said, "Hurry, and do just as you proposed. Take a garment and a horse for Mordecai the Jew, who is sitting at the King's Gate. Do not leave out anything you have suggested" (v. 10).

I'm sure you could have heard a pin drop in that royal room.

Haman had gone to the king to ask if he could kill the same man the king just ordered him to honor. Haman's planned public display of brutality against Mordecai got flipped on a dime to an even more public display of favor.

Pay attention to this because it highlights one of the areas of God's sovereignty and providence we often overlook. God is a God of intersections. He connects things that don't look connectable. He twists things that appear set in stone. He maneuvers through the maze of what appear to be unrelated occurrences. Because we can only see what is right before our eyes, we rarely get a glimpse of how He works. But it is in narratives like this one where, even with His name removed from the book, God offers a full view of who He is and how He orchestrates His will.

God always has a plan in play, even though He often speaks to us in ways we don't always recognize. That's why when there is no spiritual prioritization in your life, you will often fail to pick up on the signals that are all around you. When the receiver is off the hook, you can't answer the call. You can't connect the dots. You can't see the forest through the trees.

> *God always has a plan in play, even though He often speaks to us in ways we don't always recognize.*

One of the main ways God answers our prayers and directs us on His providential pathway is through things we consider to be coincidences. When we fail to recognize that what we *just so happened* to come across, or the person we *just so happened* to run into, or the concept we *just so happened* to get in our minds, or the certain place we *just so happened* to be in at a certain time, didn't *just so happen* after all, we set ourselves up for the risk of missing out on God's leading and provision in our lives. Providence means God intentionally stops, starts, delays, quickens, directs, moves, changes, allows, blocks, and everything else He does in His sovereign plan. And He does so on purpose. He does so because He is intersecting people, thoughts, and processes toward His intended aim. We see this all throughout the stories of Scripture.

For example, in 1 Samuel 9 we find Saul's father telling him to go out and chase down some rogue donkeys. In biblical days, donkeys were the U-Hauls of their culture. Donkeys were essential for life, work, and worship. When you lost your donkeys, you lost your access to much of what life entails. So Saul's dad sent his son out to retrieve them.

But as Saul wandered about looking for the family donkeys, he got down in the dumps. He couldn't find the donkeys. He wanted to go home. He didn't want his dad to worry anymore either because they had been gone for so long. However, when Saul's servant saw his countenance fall and heard his request to go home, he urged him to go and see a prophet instead.

Now, you might be wondering—like most people reading this story in the Bible—what does a prophet have to do with finding donkeys? Nothing, actually. At least nothing that we can see. But God operates in the spiritual realm, not in the physical. What the servant was urging Saul to do was to check with the spiritual before simply reacting to how he felt in the physical.

Similarly, we must always view the spiritual first.

Saul may have felt odd going to see a prophet about some lost donkeys. But he went anyway at the advice of his servant, only to discover that God had a surprise up His sleeve. God had already told the prophet the day before that when some random man comes to you tomorrow, anoint that man as king.

Yes, you read that right. "When some random man stops in tomorrow," God told the prophet Samuel in my Evans translation, "he's king."

Did you see the progression in circumstances?

Saul's donkeys got lost. Saul went to look for his donkeys. Saul couldn't find his donkeys. Saul wanted to go home. Saul's servant encouraged him to go see some prophet instead. Saul agreed. Saul got anointed king.

Now, I know that approach wouldn't be taught in any career-advancement seminar or on any college campus in the entire world. Because that strategy would only work for one man—the man God providentially chose in that situation to lead, guide, and connect.

> *God allows roadblocks for a reason.*

Saul wound up as king because someone whispered in his ear that maybe he should go meet with a prophet.

When things don't look like they are going anywhere—when you feel tired, worn out, and like you are having a useless day—always remember to check the spiritual first. God allows roadblocks for a reason. The Bible is replete with roadblocks, detours, U-turns, and intersections.

Another example is Ruth. Ruth *just so happened* to be gleaning in the fields, working with the leftover sheaves and looking for anything she could turn into a meal. She *just so happened* to be living in a country far from her own culture and race. She *just so happened* to attract the gaze of a man named Boaz who owned the field in which she gleaned. Out of that intersection, a widow who had never had any children got married again and had a child. That child's name is Obed. Obed later married and his wife gave birth to Jesse. Jesse married and his wife gave birth to David, who later became King David, in whose lineage Jesus would one day come to earth. Now, that's called gleaning at the right time (Ruth 2)! God has a way of connecting things right when they need to be connected.

Moses's mother put him in a basket and placed him on the Nile River because it was a dangerous time for Jewish baby boys. It *just so happened* that Pharaoh's own daughter would be bathing nearby and would wind up adopting Moses. Wasn't Moses *lucky* that his mom put him in a basket at just the right time? Wasn't Moses *lucky* that Pharaoh's daughter was bathing nearby, rather than some slave in Pharaoh's house? Wasn't Moses *lucky* that he became adopted into the royal family so that he would later be able to deliver his people from the dominant oppression of Egypt (Exod. 2:1–10)?

No, Moses wasn't lucky at all. Moses was a child of providence because that's how God works. Providence is God hooking things up in ways humanity could have never known to connect on our own.

The only reason I pastor at the location where I do today is because several decades ago, I *just so happened* to be talking with a man in his office and sharing how we didn't have the $200,000 needed to buy this property. A new congregation still struggling to meet our bills, we didn't even have $2,000. But it *just so happened* as I was sharing my discouragement with a friend that another man, whom I had never met, *just so happened* to walk by the door and overhear our conversation. Then that other man *just so happened* to come into the office and invite himself in on our conversation. Not long into this conversation, that other man—a man I had never met—*just so happened* to feel led to give us the entire $200,000 so we could buy the church property. Oh, how *lucky* I was that day to be at that place at the right time in order for some stranger who had the resources to overhear my conversation and pay for the property! No, friend, I wasn't lucky at all. I say that tongue-in-cheek. That's providence. That's sovereignty. That's God intersecting the pathways of people to fulfill His purpose.

What's more—sometime earlier as our new church met in a local school, the School Board had decided to ask us to leave. They had informed us of their decision ahead of time and said all that was needed was for them to confirm it with a vote. So my associate pastor, Pastor Hawkins, and I chose to drive to the school on the day of the vote in order to pray in person for God to change the vote. As we sat there praying, we noticed that the School Board seemed to be taking longer than normal. Time continued to pass so we continued to pray. After an hour or more, a School Board member came out to tell us we could stay as a church meeting there.

What had changed? Well, the two members who were opposed to us meeting there as a church *just so happened* to decide to ride together to the meeting that day. They also *just so happened* to come upon an accident while they were driving there. This accident *just so happened* to cause them to be delayed. By the time they arrived at the meeting, the vote had been taken and it was 5–4 in our favor to stay.

Now, some people would call that luck. Some people would call that fate. But you've got to know Who you are dealing with! That's neither luck nor fate. That is God, the Creator of the Universe stopping two men from reaching a meeting He didn't want them to attend. This same God hung every single star in the sky and somehow miraculously keeps the earth in its orbit, and provides enough oxygen for each of us to consume. If the world itself relied on *luck* for seasons, weather, and nutrients to grow its life, we'd be in a sorry situation in under a second.

This same God who providentially provides order to all in the natural realm likewise providentially intersects, arranges, sets up, steers around, and prepares your pathway with what He desires to do both in you and through you for His will and His glory.

Do you realize that it had been many years since Mordecai had saved the king's life? Mordecai had risked his own safety to speak up about an issue that threatened the king. What's more, once he did speak up about it, the king just went about his business and didn't even give Mordecai the affirmation he deserved. But that's often how God works. God sees those things you've done in years past that other people have forgotten about. God sees that thing you think was ignored, missed, or went for nothing. On God's clock, there is no boundary of time. He knows how to reach back into the past as if the past were also the present and bring that thing back up at just the right moment in order to accomplish His plan for the future.

Nothing ever goes to waste in God's economy. No kind deed you perform. No devotion or sacrifice you show to Him. God keeps a record of all you do and is a rewarder of faith, as well as actions (Col. 3:23–24; Heb. 11:6; Gal. 6:9). It may not take place in the timeframe you expect it to, and some rewards will not take place until heaven, but one thing I can assure you—God is both just and faithful.

And He sees you.

Just like He saw Mordecai. When Mordecai faced his hour of greatest need—a day in which Haman plotted to have him publicly hung, God flipped the situation on a dime. In the end, Haman wound up leading Mordecai through the city square while proclaiming to anyone and everyone within earshot that the king had chosen to honor Mordecai. If that's not called "making your enemies your footstool" (Luke 20:43), I don't know what is.

Friend, that's why you can't allow yourself to get all shook up when it looks like the devil has gotten his people in charge over you. Because when you tap into God's sovereignty and align yourself under His rule, God can change things in a moment. He can turn things around. He turned Mordecai's situation around in less than twenty-four hours. On the very day the man is supposed to die, he winds up riding on the king's horse through town!

See, when God is ready to move, He doesn't need a lot of time. God can move *suddenly*. What's more, He doesn't need anyone's help. This is because, in His providence, God can take those things that were even meant to harm you, defeat you, discourage you, or keep you from moving forward and He can use them to usher you into your destiny.

God is always at work when circumstances look uncontrollable. God is always at work when life appears to be unpredictable. God is always at work when sin looks unstoppable. In fact, God is even at work when you are asleep (Ps. 127:2). He may be silent, but He is not still. The Bible says, "When a person's ways please the LORD, he makes even his enemies to be at peace with him" (Prov. 16:7). God can flip the script in an instant.

As long as you have a small view of God or as long as you refuse to put the spiritual first (Matt. 6:33), then you are left to figure and sort things out on your own. God has all the answers, but when your spiritual receiver is off, you don't get to see the big picture. He won't plant thoughts, new ideas, or solutions in your mind when you choose to keep your mind stuck in the secular way of thinking. Rather, we have each been called to "renew" our minds so that He can transform us, and all that is attached to or around us (Rom. 12:2).

You know what the worst part of this whole story was for Haman? Not only did he get a demotion that he himself helped to arrange by having to lead around a different man in the position of highest honor in the land—on the king's horse and in the king's robe. But the worst part is that the very man he was leading was the same man he wanted to kill. What's more—he represented a race of people whom Haman loathed. This was a racist hate that drove Haman to want Mordecai dead. And yet this same man whom he had thought—just twenty-four hours earlier—that he had control over, could push around, could determine his fate, was now in a position of power on that day even higher than his own.

God does know how to level the playing field, doesn't He?

God's Providence in Addressing Racism

In fact, the providence of God can even address racism.

I don't talk about this often but I want to share it here because it is such a powerful testament to God's power to reverse situations. The year was 1969, and I was twenty years old. Not only was I a young black man during the heart of the civil rights era of unrest, but I was also a young black man living in the heart of racism itself. I had moved from Baltimore to the Deep South to attend college.

The name of the church that one of my white professors had asked me to visit with him doesn't need to be said, nor the location. I'm not trying to call them out. But attending that day with my white professor, I had no idea that anything could go wrong. As

I walked into that church, I could feel the air grow thick. I could feel the stares bore through my skin. And when I went forward at the end of the service for a personal commitment to discipleship, all hell broke loose.

See, at that time, blacks weren't allowed to attend most white churches. My professor didn't agree with that, though, and had asked me to go despite that cultural norm in the South. This decision of his wasn't received well, as you might imagine. In fact, I was told to leave and to never come back.

What's more, the church leaders later held a meeting about what their official position was going to be on this subject of "race." This meeting then led to a church split among the leaders and congregation.

On top of that, on the very Sunday I had attended, there was a guest preacher who was a candidate for the role of pastor at this church. He had been chosen to be the next pastor but they were still going through the formalities of voting. Yet after he saw what they did to me, he pulled his application and told them he would not pastor a racist church.

Years passed after this church split and they lost the pastor who had been called there at one point to preach. The church just continued to decline not only in attendees but also in impact. Eventually it became what most would consider a glorified Bible study of just a few people attending. It's as if God Himself had removed His hand. And when God removes His hand, the path you were once on is over. His providence opens doors—and closes them.

The church dissipated into disrepair.

A few years ago, I got an interesting phone call from the Chairman of the Deacon Board of this church. A quiet voice on the other end of the line said, "Tony, our church has never recovered from that day you came to visit with your professor."

I didn't know what to say, so I just said, "Sorry to hear that, but I understand."

He continued, "And we recognize the reason God has not answered our prayers or rebuilt this church is because of the racist acts we did to you back in 1969, as well as to so many others. So, Tony, I've been asked on behalf of the Deacons to call you to apologize for the racism we had against you. I am also calling you to humbly request if you would come and preach at our church."

The same church who wouldn't allow me to attend was now asking me to preach.

God *is* the God of reversals.

The same man who had set out to hang Mordecai on gallows was now leading him around town on the king's horse.

God *is* the God of reversals.

The same God who sovereignly intervened to flip the script on both situations is also the same God who knows how to address whatever it is you are facing, or whomever it is you have faced. He can tweak it, twist it, flip it, and reverse it for your good and His glory (Rom. 8:28).

He *is* the God of reversals.

If you will simply let go of the pain that comes from confusion, release the distrust that arises from the dust of disappointments, and replace both with trust in the providential heart of God, you will see Him reverse things in your life you thought could never change. Like Mordecai, like Esther, like me, you will see Him turn things around, on a dime.

God *is* the God of divine reversals.

CHAPTER EIGHT

Suddenly

 Trying to figure out God is like trying to put together a five-billion-piece puzzle. Actually, it's more like trying to put together five different five-billion-piece puzzles that have been mixed together. It's just too many pieces with too many variations. His thoughts are not our thoughts and His ways are not our ways (Isa. 55:8–9). Our finite minds simply cannot figure out an infinite Being. It's a waste of our time to try and outsmart Him, outwit Him, or outmaneuver Him.

And while God has certainly revealed a lot about Himself to us in His Word and through the course of our lives, as Deuteronomy 29:29 reminds us, He still holds His cards close to His chest in many ways: "The secret things belong to the Lord our God . . ." (NASB). Yes, He's given us a glimpse into His overwhelming existence—a peek at His hind parts like Moses saw (Exod. 33:23)—but most of who He is and the bulk of what He does, and can do, remains elusive. It remains out of our ability to understand.

Did you know that one drop of water contains 1.67 sextillion molecules? I would be surprised if you knew that since that's not information most of us walk around discussing. But you can confirm it if you'd like. Google it. It's accurate. One tiny drop of water contains a number of molecules that none of us are even able to count, were we to try. Try counting to 1.67 sextillion sometime and let me know how far you get.

What's more, if you were to multiply that number—a number which none of us have the available time to even count—by three, you would have the number of atoms in a drop of water. That number is 5,012,489,600,000,000,000,000. Yes, that's a real number. It would take a month just to figure out how to say it right.

But just know that when you or I fill up a glass of water to drink, we are filling that cup with an abundance of drops—each of which contain roughly 5,012,489,600,000,000,000,000 atoms. Or, if you were to look out over a river, a pond, lake, sea, or ocean—you could multiply all of those drops by the number of atoms in each drop in order to find out how many atoms there are in there too. It becomes too much for a mind to grasp. And yet if God were to lose track of just one solitary atom, He would no longer be God. If one atom were to go astray, creation would come apart at the seams.

Or, take the hair on your head. The average person is born with over 100,000 hair follicles on their head. Sure, some wind up with a large number of those hair follicles no longer producing hair by middle age, but we all get a fair start. Now, multiply that average number of hair follicles by seven billion people on the planet and you're now in the octillion range of mathematical computation. When most of us think of octillion, we think of that slimy creature living in the sea—not a number so far beyond our natural ability to compute. And yet God says that not one solitary hair falls from your head with which He is not fully acquainted (Luke 12:7; Matt. 10:30).

And this very God, who doesn't miss a microsecond or simple syllable on any subject known to humanity, is so brilliant in His capacity that He can take things that appear to be totally unrelated, disconnected, and random—and make sense out of them. God can put a billion-piece puzzle together in less time than it takes you to blink. He is so much bigger than we often give Him credit for. He is so much more able than we often even realize. He is so much more sovereign in the daily workings of our lives than we often dare to fathom.

It is this very greatness of God that you need most when life has become a mess. It is this strategic sovereignty that you must rely on when life no longer makes sense. It is this control by our Creator that you must trust when circumstances appear chaotic. Sometimes the bigness and sovereignty of God can scare us, as if a God so big doesn't have time to care about our little lives. But by the grace of God in Jesus, we are children of the King. And as children of the King, we are called to believe in this doctrine of sovereignty— also known as superintendence—because that is how we live by faith. We are asked to believe in this God who strings together the incomprehensible in order to make sense of the senseless in those times when things are no longer going our way. In order to work all things together for our good.

Unfortunately, though, what we often do when things appear to be spiraling out of control is to take matters into our own hands instead. We seek to control our own circumstances.

Yet this only causes more mess.

I understand why we do this. I'm not casting stones, just overturning them in all of us. It's easy to feel in uncertain times that if you don't take care of it, it won't be taken care of. It's easy to think that the health report, financial situation, relationship struggle, or stalling career won't change unless you force it to change. And yet, the wisdom found in a finite mind comprised of an ability to see only what has happened or is happening, will never be enough wisdom to truly know the best route to take. That would be like asking you or me to hold those 5,012,489,600,000,000,000,000 atoms in that droplet of water in place. It's beyond our scope of skills.

> *We seek to control our own circumstances. Yet this only causes more mess.*

That's why the kingdom life requires faith. Faith is trusting that what God says is true, even when you cannot understand it or see the connecting points between what He says. Faith is taking steps that demonstrate what He has said is true. It is acting like something is so, even when it is not so, in order that it might be so simply because God said so. Faith requires risk beyond reason out of a trust that God knows what He is doing.

The only book of the Bible that doesn't mention God by name has His fingerprints all over it. As a result, it has this element of faith interwoven throughout it. As we have already seen, Esther has discovered that she has been placed in her position for a spiritual reason, not merely for a personal benefit. She has been called to the kingdom "for such a time as this." She has learned that God's whole plan in making her pretty was so that she would be chosen out of all the possible females in the kingdom to become the queen. God's whole plan in creating her character was so that she would fulfill the kingdom purpose in store for her. God's entire plan in positioning her as royalty was so she could save an entire group of people from annihilation. God orchestrated each movement, moment, and early-morning conversation to converge into a masterpiece of meaning.

Providential Timing

Esther had prepared the first banquet for the king and his right-hand man, the architect of genocide himself, Haman. When the king had asked her what she wanted, she paused. She delayed. She postponed the request once again. This was the second time she had postponed answering his question about what she needed. The first time came in the inner court where she bravely approached the throne and he held out the golden scepter.

When the king asked Esther following the first dinner what she wanted, she chose to delay her petition. She chose to push back the pronouncement of her need. She chose to invite him and Haman back for another banquet. The timing of this shouldn't be overlooked or downplayed, because it was in between the first banquet and the second, on the very next night, that a myriad of critical things occurred. There were a number of things God wanted to happen to set the stage for Esther's request. If Esther had impulsively jumped ahead of God's leading and asked the king for what she wanted in the inner court, or at the first banquet, she would have turned down the wrong path.

See, timing matters to God. He does things with such precision that following His lead and aligning under His direction is imperative to progressing on His providential pathway for your life. Let me explain something about God. God not only wants you to do the right thing—the thing He is asking you to do—but He wants you to do the right thing at the right time. He has an exquisitely intricate, woven schematic of circumstances interplaying and interlinking at such a high level of connectivity that, like one atom gone astray, we can miss out on the plans He desires for us when we balk under His leading.

When Esther allowed the intermission to occur between Dinner One and Dinner Two, she gave space for God to continue arranging the plot. Haman left her presence and ran across Mordecai.

Mordecai refused to bow and angered Haman. Haman complained to his friends and family. His friends and family encouraged him to kill Mordecai the very next day. Haman agreed that was a very good plan and would solve his problem once and for all.

The king went to bed but could not sleep. While the king was tossing and turning, he got the idea to have a big, boring book read to him. They brought the king his book of chronicles and read about the man named Mordecai saving his life by revealing a plan to take it. The king inquired as to what was done for Mordecai. Haman walked in while the king was inquiring. The king asked Haman what should be done to honor someone. Mordecai offered an elaborate plan. The king accepted, charging Haman to honor Mordecai with his own concocted plan. Haman led Mordecai through the streets on the king's horse wearing the king's robe for all eyes to see.

Friend, it was Esther's willingness to pause between the dinners which produced the delay, which produced the movement, which produced Mordecai's rejection, which produced Haman building gallows, which produced a sleepless night, which produced a boring book, which produced the revelation of a hero, which produced Haman having to honor the man he had hoped to hang.

God—the Puppet-Master—pulled all things together to bring about His timing for His providential plan. In order for that to happen, though—in order for there to be time to set the stage for the change of scenery—God had to have someone willing to trust Him with a pause. He had to have someone willing to not rush

ahead and try to solve the problem herself. He had to have someone who, when asked what she wanted up to half of an entire kingdom, could stick to the plan and simply say, "I want you to come
back for dinner once again."

He needed someone who was willing to submit personal strategy to His Spirit's rule.

Following the Leader

The job of the Holy Spirit is to release you or restrict you from
movement. God has a beeper system inside every believer who is in
contact with Him. Fellowship with the Holy Spirit enables you to
be led by Him about what you are to do and what you are not to
do, and when. Because with God, it's all about timing. That's why
we read time and time again things like:

The Spirit told me to accompany them . . . (Acts 11:12)

. . . they had been forbidden by the Holy Spirit to speak the
word in Asia. (Acts 16:6)

. . . but the Spirit of Jesus did not allow them. (Acts 16:7)

That is why I have been prevented many times from coming to
you. (Rom. 15:22)

The Holy Spirit is there to direct not only what we do but also
when we do it. It's when God won't give you the freedom to move
forward on something, or when you are feeling a nudge to move

forward more quickly than you thought. When something seems to be holding you back from saying what you felt right then and there. Or when you feel led to say something you never thought you would. The Spirit gives the freedom or the restriction we need to remain on the path of God's will.

Yet if you do not have a spiritual antenna connected to God's presence, you won't pick up His leading. You won't know which step to take and when to take it. That's why the Bible says that only those who are spiritual will be able to perceive such things (1 Cor. 2:14–16).

If you choose to live with a worldview rooted in secular thinking, you will be messing up God's program for your life because you will be moving when He doesn't want you to move, or not moving when He does want you to move. You will be speaking when He doesn't want you to speak, or not speaking when He does want you to speak. If you cannot discern how to pick up heaven's signal because your receiver is turned off, you will not know which step to take or which direction to turn. It would be like trying to hike up a mountain at night without a light—dangerous, disastrous, and deadly. The Holy Spirit's work in your life is to illuminate God's guidance as you travel upon this journey called life.

One of the main reasons you and I need the Holy Spirit's illumination is because God often acts counterintuitively to how we think and plan. There are many times when God uses negatives to accomplish positives. He will use what appears to be something bad in order to bring about something good. He even uses the devil to achieve His righteous goals. And if He's willing to use the devil to bring about His intended outcomes, then you know He's also willing to use devilish people to do the same.

But if you don't know that, and I mean *truly* know that, when those times occur that you get hit by the devil or one of his minions, then you will wind up reacting to what you can see. You will wind up emoting on what you perceive. You will wind up traveling in the direction of fixing what you know how to fix, all the while messing up God's perfect plan.

The narrative of Esther is designed to show us that even when God is nowhere to be found—His name never once appears in the book—and even when all things appear to be converging into a perfect storm, God is operating behind the scenes and situations in order to move things forward to accomplish His will. Because God has to work with finite minds like ours who are always trying to one-up Him, out-smart Him, and counter-maneuver Him, He oftentimes has to resort to pressure or pull to get us where we need to go.

There was a sergeant in the Army once who was working out his men in order to see how far they progressed. One part of the workout regimen called for the men to run to a bank of water and leap over it while not getting wet. The men set out to jump and a few made it over, but most of the men wound up partially or entirely in the water.

The sergeant informed the men that their failure was simply unacceptable. He told them that early the next morning they would be back at this bank to jump over it once again. "This time," the sergeant said sternly, "you will make it over."

The men woke up early the next morning and made their way to the bank, only to discover that the sergeant had filled the water with hungry alligators. Yes, all the men somehow managed to jump the entirety of the water this time.

Sometimes God will allow a bad situation, dangerous scenario, or unpredictable problem to swim into your world in order to take you to a place you would never naturally make on your own. This pain and pressure placed on the pathway of life propels you to a greater level of effort, focus, zest, power, and piety you'd ever accomplish on your own.

Yet if you don't know that, or if you don't understand that God works in ways that involve difficulties and disasters, you'll grow cynical, untrusting, and fearful instead. The book of Esther was recorded to show you and me that God does not orchestrate things in a normal fashion. It is not a regular occurrence for Him to succinctly work things out straightforwardly. Rather, He weaves as we wait. He positions as we pause. He maneuvers as we move. Then, when the time comes as it did with Esther, He sets the stage—suddenly. In less than twenty-four hours, God flipped the script and the curtain rose on a brand-new scene.

Oh, how I love that word *suddenly*. Throughout Scripture, God moved suddenly to arrange, rearrange, and promote His plan into place. Waiting on God means we are waiting on Him to put things together in the perfect timing for things to happen. It doesn't mean we are waiting on Him to construct everything. Rather, we are waiting on Him to arrange all of the pieces, places, and people in the plan. God is a God of *suddenly* (2 Chron. 29:36; Acts 16:25–26).

Friend, I wish I could tell you how much longer you are going to have to wait for your change to come. I wish I could tell you how much longer they are going to be disrespecting you or overlooking you on your job. I wish I could tell you how much longer you are going to be treated badly in that situation you face. I wish I knew how long the waiting game would be in the plan of God. But I do not. I cannot tell you how long because there are too many pieces of the puzzle. There are too many people on the pathway. There are too many processes in the plan.

But what I can tell you is that when God does show up, it will often come about suddenly. And in such an unexpected way. God often lets things get worse before they get better. Sometimes He will allow you to go all the way to the end—to hit rock bottom, so that you will discover that He is the Rock at the bottom. In doing so, He builds our faith muscles and strengthens our spirit. He also gets the glory and the praise because only He can produce a miracle out of a mess.

> *God often lets things get worse before they get better.*

I'll never forget several decades ago when we were just a young couple, trying to get by in seminary. We were committed to my wife staying home to raise the kids and not working during those years, so I was trying to go to school full-time while also trying to earn enough for food and rent. Yet even working as much as I could, burning the candle at both ends, we were barely getting by.

One morning as I sat down to do our daily devotions as a couple, I noticed that my wife began to cry. Her heart had hit a low point. All we had in the cabinets were some beans. All we had in the fridge were some hot dogs. All we had to drink was some coffee. I knew that this wasn't what it meant for a husband to "provide," so I asked her what she needed for me to be able to stay in school. I asked her how much she needed by way of food, or anything else. And I promised her that if we didn't get what she needed—no matter what she said the amount was—by the end of that very day, I would drop out of school, and work even more to provide for our young family.

The words came quickly and softly from her mouth, "$500, Tony. We need $500."

That was a lot of money in the mid-1970s. But we were behind on rent, our car barely made it anywhere we needed to go, and we had no food. She was right. So I drove to seminary that day with a prayer on my lips, "Lord, please give us $500 or show me Your plan. I thought You had called me to seminary but You have also called me to provide for my family, and right now, I'm not able to do both."

Lo and behold, when I got to seminary that day, I walked over to my student mailbox and opened it up. Inside the mailbox was an unmarked envelope. No return address. No name other than mine.

And inside were five $100 bills. There weren't six of them. There weren't four. There were five because $500 is what my wife had said we needed for me to stay in school. God was making a point. This was Him reversing human circumstances *suddenly* in accordance with His will.

Years later the man who had given us that money introduced himself and told me what had happened. He explained how God had put my name on his mind, and specifically told him to give me $500 that very day. God led, and even though this man didn't know where this leading was going, he obeyed. He didn't know why he felt urged to do it that very day and not to delay it. He didn't even know me, other than by name. I had never spoken to him before in my life. But let me explain how God works. God can whisper in someone's ear in order to answer a prayer that someone is praying elsewhere. He can reach far and wide to connect things nearby, in order to let you know that He has everything under control. He can come through for you in the nick of time.

Yes, God often allows us to get backed into a corner so that we no longer know what is going on or how to solve it. He does so in order for us to discover that He alone is God. But if your spiritual antenna is not up—if you are thinking worldly, living worldly, and making decisions based on your own insight, you won't be able to pick up the signals of His Spirit. You'll miss the leading which is necessary to take you along the pathway of providence.

CHAPTER NINE

Divine Reversals

 We pick up Esther's story by cuing onto the stage a very depressed man. If this were a musical, he'd belt out a franticly sad ballad. Haman is in a very low point emotionally because he was leading around the streets a man whom he had wanted to hang. So when he gets home, he begins to cry and mourn with his head covered.

Haman's wife doesn't help the situation. She starts to complain and nag him as well. Yet while his wife and friends are telling him that things don't look good for him, something else happens. The king's eunuchs arrive at precisely the same moment of this conversation. In fact, the verse begins with the telling word *while*. Keep in mind, *while* is a timing-based word. Why is that important? Because timing always matters in God's providential plans.

We read: "While they were still speaking with him, the king's eunuchs arrived and rushed Haman to the banquet Esther had prepared" (Esther 6:14). Now, this is the second banquet. This is the second dinner. This is part of the plan God placed in Esther's heart to delay her request to the king until He indicated it was the right moment. And because of this delay in the request, we now have an entirely different situation at hand.

Just twenty-four hours have reset the stage. Haman is now caught off guard. Mordecai has been exalted publicly. Haman didn't have time to concoct another plan on what to do against Mordecai because as he was talking with his family and friends, he was swiftly taken to the second banquet. In short, Haman's world has been turned upside down and he's not had the time to figure out how to get it back right again.

Thus, as the three of them dine once again, the king extends his offer to Esther once more. Up to half of the kingdom is hers, simply for the asking. Her moment has come. Her opportunity to speak has presented itself. Esther locates the courage within and voices her need clearly this time, laying it all out on the table:

> "If I have found favor in your eyes, Your Majesty, and if the king is pleased, spare my life; this is my request. And spare my people; this is my desire. For my people and I have been sold to destruction, death, and extermination. If we had merely been sold as male and female slaves, I would have kept silent. Indeed, the trouble wouldn't be worth burdening the king." (Esther 7:3–4)

156

The king is alarmed. Shocked. Angered. He asks Esther who would have come up with such a terrible idea and plan. Esther responds pointedly. Unsure of the outcome of what she was about to say, I imagine her voice may have been shaky as well, "The adversary and enemy is this evil Haman" (Esther 7:6).

Haman, the very man sitting at the dinner table with them. Haman, the very man whom the king involved in matters of nation and matters of defense. Haman, the very man the king trusted. But because she mentions this on the second dinner and not on the first, it's also now Haman—the very man who had built gallows for Mordecai but had to honor Mordecai instead. There had been a crack in his character revealed to the king. There had been fear in his spirit placed there by such a sudden change of events the day before. God waited to release Esther to tell the king when the time was right for her to do so. Because of this, the king doesn't even question Esther. Rather, he immediately becomes enraged. He's so angry that he cannot even talk. Scripture tells us that he stormed out into the palace gardens.

While he's outside trying to get a grip on his emotions, Haman foolishly approaches Esther to beg for his life. Yet timing comes into play once again. Because we read that as Haman was begging for his life, the king returned into the room. It says:

> Just as the king returned from the palace garden to the banquet hall, Haman was falling on the couch where Esther was reclining. Then the king exclaimed, "Would he actually violate the queen while I am in the house?" As soon as

the statement left the king's mouth, they covered Haman's face. (Esther 7:8)

I can imagine that as the king saw what he saw, still hot from his rage, he had to be thinking, "You have got to be kidding me! Haman, you already told me that you want to kill my wife and now you are all over her in my own home, assaulting her in my house?" If the king's hatred for Haman hadn't reached full capacity before he left to go outside, it was beyond his boiling point upon returning.

What's more, Haman wasn't actually assaulting Esther. He was begging for his life. But God is so good at being the providential God that He is, He will even allow impressions to take place of things that aren't really happening—in order to accomplish His will. God is so nuanced that He will make something look like it's taking place simply to bring about His intended aim. Which is exactly what this impression brought about. As soon as the king saw Haman in a position that appeared to him as one of assault, his servants immediately covered Haman's face. They didn't allow him even a moment to speak for himself. God didn't provide an opportunity for Haman to defend himself. This is because when God acts in judgment against an enemy of His will, He often acts swiftly.

Not only did the servants cover his face, but they also suggested that they hang him on the gallows he'd built for Mordecai. The king didn't need any time at all to think about that decision. He told them to hang Haman on it right then.

God had delayed Esther from telling the king the first two times he'd asked what she wanted from him. Had Esther impulsively gone ahead of God's timing, then Haman wouldn't have become angry at Mordecai and he wouldn't have built the gallows upon which he would now be hanged. Obeying God's divine timing allowed Haman to dig his own grave.

God will allow unbelievers or enemies of His will to express their anger in order that He might use that very thing to stop that person from carrying out the destruction they had intended. It's all got to do with time. It's got to do with God nuancing time.

The God of Reversals

God is a God of reversals. He can reverse things quickly that appear to be irreversible. In the chapter 8 of Esther, we discover a number of these reversals. The first one is that the king gave the house of Haman, the enemy of the Jews, to Queen Esther (v. 1). That's called an economic reversal, a reversal of fortune. All that Haman owned now belonged to Esther. Scripture says, ". . . the sinner's wealth is stored up for the righteous" (Prov. 13:22). When God gets ready to make a statement in the economic order of things, He can flip things entirely around for you. He doesn't need much time to do it either. All that Haman owned was now Esther's. Haman was a rich man. He had put up all of that money and was going to use a portion of it to kill the Jews. But now the king had placed it all in the hands of a certain Jew, Esther.

Not only that, we also see a reversal of power. This was a political reversal. In verse 2 we read, "The king removed his signet ring he had recovered from Haman and gave it to Mordecai, and Esther put him in charge of Haman's estate." The signet ring was a ring of authority. It was a ring that indicated power, prowess, and rule. Now, rather than Haman having the king's authority to wield over whomever he pleased, this had been stripped from him and given to Mordecai. Mordecai could now represent the king officially. Mordecai carried clout. He carried class. His station in life had changed in an instant. This same man who just two days before was a dead-man walking is now second-in-command wearing the king's own signet ring.

Friend, God can change your circumstances with the flip of a switch. You may think that your boss has the final say. You may think "the powers-that-be" have the final say. You may think that those unscrupulous coworkers who are plotting against you have the final say. You may think that because they have the name, the money, the position, or the power that what they say goes. But the truth is, they do not have a thing unless God gives it to them. What's more, the God who gives it can also take it away. If you don't believe me, ask Nebuchadnezzar.

King Nebuchadnezzar stood over his domain of Babylon and said, "Is this not Babylon the Great that I have built to be a royal residence by my vast power and for my majestic glory?" (Dan. 4:30). Essentially, he declared that he was the man. He was the boss. He was the head honcho in charge. All revolved around him.

That didn't sit so well with God, so God let King Nebuchadnezzar know just how much power he really did have. The next part of the passage begins with that important word we noticed earlier, *while*. *While* denotes timing. It says:

> While the words were still in the king's mouth, a voice came from heaven: "King Nebuchadnezzar, to you it is declared that the kingdom has departed from you. You will be driven away from people to live with the wild animals, and you will feed on grass like cattle for seven periods of time, until you acknowledge that the Most High is ruler over human kingdoms, and he gives them to anyone he wants."
>
> At that moment the message against Nebuchadnezzar was fulfilled. He was driven away from people. He ate grass like cattle, and his body was drenched with dew from the sky, until his hair grew like eagles' feathers and his nails like birds' claws.
>
> But at the end of those days, I, Nebuchadnezzar, looked up to heaven, and my sanity returned to me. Then I praised the Most High and honored and glorified him who lives forever:
>
> > For his dominion is an everlasting dominion,
> > and his kingdom is from generation to generation.
> > All the inhabitants of the earth are counted as
> > > nothing,

and he does what he wants with the army of heaven
and the inhabitants of the earth.
There is no one who can block his hand
or say to him, "What have you done?"

At that time my sanity returned to me, and my majesty
and splendor returned to me for the glory of my kingdom.
(Dan. 4:31–36a)

King Nebuchadnezzar learned very quickly whose dominion and kingdom is really in control. For seven years, God reduced this powerful man to be nothing more than an animal out in the field. When his reason finally returned to him, he let everyone know that God, and God alone, rules, and it is according to His will that nations are lifted up or brought down low.

The point is simple: there is only one Source. If you can ever get this truth deep down into your gizzard, into the very heart of your being, you will be set free from worry and stress. Nobody—and I don't care who they are—has the final say-so over you as a Christian who lives by the Spirit in the will of God. Nobody. Which means that you never have to live afraid. You never have to live a threatened life.

> *Man does not have the final say. God does.*

Yes, I understand that things may look threatening to you, but you never have to view them as they look because man does not have the final say. God does.

162

Not only did God provide a reversal of fortunes and a reversal of power in Esther's story, but He also created a legal shift. God reversed the legal rights and restrictions of an entire group of people. Esther asked the king for him to revoke the letters devised by Haman for the Jews to be killed. And while the king did not have the power to revoke what he had already set in motion, he did provide an alternative plan. He instructed his scribes to write according to Mordecai's commands for defending themselves against the attack on their lives. These letters were then dispersed among all the inhabitants in the land near and far, in enough time for them to plan their counterattack.

We read: "The king's edict gave the Jews in each and every city the right to assemble and defend themselves, to destroy, kill, and annihilate every ethnic and provincial army hostile to them, including women and children, and to take their possessions as spoils of war. This would take place on a single day throughout all the provinces of King Ahasuerus, on the thirteenth day of the twelfth month, the month Adar" (Esther 8:11–12).

According to Haman's law, every Jew was going to be killed. This law couldn't be changed. So the king told Esther to come up with another plan and put his seal on it, and he would also make it law. He wrote an executive order that all Jews now had the right to defend themselves against anyone who tried to kill them on that predetermined day.

Now, if I'm a Persian operating under the premise of law number one where the Jews cannot defend themselves, but then I find out that they can now kill me and my family in return, and collect our belongings as their own spoils—I'm going to rethink this entire plan. I'm going to rethink whether or not I even want to take part. Especially when the order was from the king himself.

God has an override button that can take what Satan has set in place against you—it can even take people who have raised themselves up against you, or circumstances that are clearly not in your favor—and when He pushes the override button, He provides a way out. It may not stop their evil from being evil, but it can boomerang that evil right back at them rather than at you so that you come out ahead when all is said and done. Isaiah 59:19 says, "When the enemy shall come in like a flood, the Spirit of the Lord shall lift up a standard against him" (kjv). He will push the override button.

Thus far, we've seen an economic reversal, a political reversal, a legal reversal, and now there is also an emotional reversal. If you remember in Esther 4:3, "There was great mourning among the Jewish people . . . They fasted, wept, and lamented, and many lay in sackcloth and ashes." That's when the first law was passed. But when the second law was passed and the carriers sent the message to the Jews that they could defend themselves, we read in Esther 8:16–17a, "And the Jews celebrated with gladness, joy, and honor. In every province and every city, wherever the king's command and his law reached, joy and rejoicing took place among the Jews. There was a celebration and a holiday."

God can do the same with you. You may be crying today, but don't think that's how it's going to be when you wake up tomorrow.

Not when God enters the situation. God can wipe tears away. He can turn pain into pleasure. He can turn sadness into joy. When you learn how to operate with His divine reversal principles and according to His leading and timing, submitting to His will and learning His voice, your emotions can be changed in an instant from despair to joy.

Oh, but it's not over yet. Because there's one more thing. The last verse of Esther chapter 8 ends with this, "And many of the ethnic groups of the land professed themselves to be Jews because fear of the Jews had overcome them" (v. 17). Don't you love that? Through the Jews' routing of their enemies and through God manifesting His power among them, many people came to the faith. When they witnessed the strength of the unseen God, the precision of the Puppet-Master, the intentionality of the invisible Hand, they wanted to be with Him. They were not foolish; they knew Whose side to be on. In that day, to become a Jew meant you had to come under the Jewish covenant. To come under the Jewish covenant, you had to accept the Jewish God.

Not only did God deliver His people through this turn of events, but He also brought many more people into His fold than before. Sometimes God allows you to be put in a negative or difficult situation so that He can give you a supernatural deliverance in order that others will witness it and come to Him. Others will see the God who flipped things around for you and they will want Him as God too. They will want God to do for them what He has done for you. There is a spiritual reversal in people's lives when they hear a testimony or catch a glimpse of what the One True God can really do.

There are many days when I wish I could be a preacher who could tell those listening that if you come to God, you will have no enemies. Or if you come to God, you will face no difficult days. If you come to God, you will have no lean years, disappointments, or bad employers. I wish I could preach that, but I can't, because I would be lying. All throughout Scripture, God allows challenges, setbacks, and negative scenarios because it is against the backdrop of impossibilities that His beauty shines through. Just like a diamond glistens most brightly when placed on the backdrop of darkness, God's glory displays brightly as He brings about divine reversals.

God's glory displays brightly as He brings about divine reversals.

The point being: Yes, you will face challenges on the pathway to your purpose. But whatever it is you come up against, it doesn't have to have the last say. When you stay tethered to the One who pulls the strings, you can witness Him come through for you in every single way.

CHAPTER TEN

Connecting the Dots

 I imagine that when you were growing up, you may have passed the time doing an activity familiar to most of us called "Dot to Dot." In this game, there is an image hidden on a page that you create by following a numbered order of connecting the dots. The number one may be on the opposite side as number two, three, or four. They are placed all over the page in random order and it's your job to draw the line that connects each one. Once you finish connecting all of the dots, you discover the image on the page. You get the picture. (Pardon the pun.)

Now, you would have never been able to guess the picture merely by looking at the numbered dots. Similarly, you can never guess God's providential destiny for your life merely by looking at the circumstances you are facing. The picture of the kingdom purpose of God is only revealed by Him causing or allowing the various situations in life until a completed image is formed.

Such is the image of Esther. We've seen God continue to connect the dots of her life in what appeared to be random occurrences over a long period of time. But as more and more of those dots become connected, we are starting to see what had at one point looked like a tragic story turn into a triumph. Recognizing the image God is creating in our own lives requires this level of attention and consistency that you would have used in the "dot to dot" activity. It also requires a perspective that is rooted in His own.

Providence Changes Your Perspective

There are areas around the world where the number of wolves outnumber the quantity of their prey. When this occurs, it's possible for the wolves to kill off an entire group of animals in their region. Thus, conservationists work to control the numbers of animals in any certain area in order to keep the population of all animals viable.

For example, in Alaska, hunters could sell wolf pelts for several hundred dollars each. At one point in time, a small bounty was also placed on each wolf by the state itself. This being so, the humorous story came about where a hunter named Bill called his friend John and informed him of the bounty. Bill asked John if he wanted to go hunting with him over the weekend. John quickly agreed and off the two men went.

They decided to camp out overnight in an area known for large packs of wolves. So they set up their tent, got their gear ready for the next day, and went to sleep. Early the next morning, Bill and John were awakened to loud sounds coming from just outside their tent. It sounded like growling. Bill grabbed the flashlight and went to look outside the tent window. As he did, his eyes grew wide. Over a hundred wolves circled their tent, teeth showing, tongues hanging out, and saliva dripping onto the cold snow beneath them. Bill shook John and yelled, "Wake up! Wake up! Wake up!"

John opened his eyes and shouted back, "What? What is it?"

Bill grinned broadly and said, "Look! We're rich!"

Friend, it's all about your perspective. Perspective is how you see what you see. Because sometimes you can be surrounded by circumstances that don't look good at all. Or there are those times when situations appear to be completely out of your favor. In fact, it can look as if they are going to devour you right then and there. But when you discern how to view life with a kingdom perspective, you will recognize the upside to every difficulty you face. With God, there is always an upside. A challenge is simply an opportunity for Him to showcase His power and might in your life.

The Red Sea wasn't certain death for the Israelites as the Egyptians chased them in six hundred chariots armed for battle. No, the Red Sea was the stage on which God performed two miracles—parting it for them to pass and also drying the ground so they wouldn't get bogged down in the mud as they walked (Exod. 14:21–22).

The fainting five thousand (not including women and children) who followed Jesus to hear Him teach despite lacking any food to eat wasn't a humanitarian disaster waiting to happen. No, feeding the five thousand from the crumbs of some bread and fish was the screen on which Jesus showcased His abilities over the natural realm, as well as His character of trust and gratitude in the presence of need and want (Matt. 14:13–21).

The planned annihilation of the Jews by a resentful, proud man named Haman wasn't the end of a people earmarked by God through whom He would bless the world. No, it was the backdrop for a saga which highlighted His providential power to reverse events, decrees, and positions with ease and precision.

Studying through the book of Esther will attack anyone's perspective on "luck." You cannot have divine providence and luck at the same time. Chance, fate, and happenstance do not exist simultaneously with God's providential hand. The providence of God means that God is in control by either causing or allowing all things.

You cannot have a sovereign God and also have Him getting caught by surprise. He's the only Being in history whom you would not be able to throw a surprise party for. What's more, God never says, "Oops." His providence is His arranging of all things to accomplish His sovereign purposes. God hooks things up to bring about whatever purpose He intends in any given situation.

If you have come to the end of this book showcasing the life of Esther and your view of God's providence has not expanded, then I have failed, because the entire book of Esther is designed to expand your view of God. It is designed to shift your perspective away from spotting the challenges and difficulties of life toward seeing the opportunities God has created to highlight His power. I've mentioned this before but it's worth repeating—nowhere in the entire book of Esther does God mention His name. He is nowhere to be overtly seen. Which makes it all the more remarkable what He brings about. And should make it all the more clear for you to recognize His fingerprints moving in your own life and in your own circumstances, even when there are no obvious ways to recognize Him.

Realizing the supreme sovereignty of God will free you from living with frustration, anxiety, and confusion. One of the major questions I get asked as a pastoral counselor is "why" God allowed this, allowed that, caused this, or brought about that . . . when it appears that things are headed south. People ask this question because when life doesn't make sense, it's easy to get mad at God. It's easy to run from the faith. It's easy to go rogue and even want to distance ourselves from God. Far

> *Realizing the supreme sovereignty of God will free you from living with frustration, anxiety, and confusion.*

too many people back away from faith when life becomes tumultuous simply due to boxing God in too tightly to their own understanding.

As you've seen from the life story of Esther, God allows evil to occur. While God does not perform evil Himself or even endorse it, He does utilize it to bring about His intended aim. Our responsibility as His children is to live with the right perspective of Him. We are to align ourselves under His rule, trusting His care so that we can pick up the signals of His leading. If Esther would have thrown a temper tantrum when she found out Haman had set out to destroy her people, we would most likely have a very different direction in this story. If Esther would have barged in to see the king uninvited and not according to God's leading, that golden scepter may not have been extended to her at that time. Living a life in tune with God's providence means staying so close to the Holy Spirit that His guidance becomes second nature to your own.

My father is one of the wisest men I've ever known. He raised me according to the principles of Scripture and instilled in me a deep love for the Word of God. When I recently asked my dad what his advice would be to a new believer, he boiled it down to two simple, yet profound, things. He said, "Study the Word of God to obey it, and follow the leading of the Holy Spirit." That's kingdom discipleship in a nutshell. Know God's Word and obey it while staying so close to His Spirit that you can discern what to say, when to say it, where to go, where not to go, and more—in order to remain on the pathway of His preferred providential direction.

The Holy Spirit is often referred to as a "dove" in Scripture. If you know anything about doves, you know that they can be a skittish bird. It doesn't take much for them to fly away. Take one step toward a dove and off it goes. In fact, a lot of birds are similar. That's why it's so critical in our relationship with the Holy Spirit to remain in alignment. We are to remain closely tied to Him in prayer, cleansed of our sins through the shed blood of Christ, and devoted in our obedience. When that happens, we discover a destiny of moving in cadence with God's carefully calculated plans.

I was preaching not long ago when a bird made its presence known in our sanctuary. Now, we've had birds in the sanctuary from time to time and, typically, the bird will eventually land somewhere while leaving everyone alone. But this bird had a mind of its own. This bird seemed to be dive-bombing the congregation, flying up and down the aisles like a stealth fighter on a mission. The bird was causing so much disruption that it caused me to stop preaching—not such an easy thing to do! But since everyone had shifted their attention to the bird, I sought to find a solution. "Could someone please catch that bird, and take it outside?" I asked the congregation, as heads continued to duck here and there, making the sanctuary look like one big whack-a-mole game.

"Really," I continued, "can someone just catch the bird? Then go and release it where it belongs." As you might imagine, there were no volunteers. I sighed, wishing I could just catch that bird myself and be done with it. That's when suddenly, just as I finished speaking those words about catching it and, as if on cue, the bird flew directly up to where I stood preaching (or in this moment, I stood pausing from preaching) and it landed a few steps away from my feet. Knowing the nature of birds, I gently walked over to it.

Then I bent down and, gently again, picked it up. The bird never moved. I then handed the bird to someone else to take outside.

The capture was in the approach. While the bird soared and flew throughout the sanctuary, everyone ducking and screaming only alarmed the bird. But when it flew to where I stood, I was able to gently move closer to it, bend down, and lift it as if nothing were changed in its environment at all.

I don't want to overstate the nature of this comparison. I am not saying the Holy Spirit is scared of us and will run away if we come close. Rather, what I am saying is that the closeness that was created with the bird in the sanctuary is the closeness that the Holy Spirit longs to have with each us. He desires us to live in such close cadence with His own environment that we are in sync with His every move.

The problems in connecting with God's providence arise when we become alarmed by life's adverse circumstances and situations. When we start hollering, moving, jumping, running, and ducking due to the fears and frets around us, we are unable to hear that still, small voice of the Spirit and embrace oneness with Him.

Yet, following the Spirit's every move is critical to progressing on the pathway of providence. Had Esther asked for Haman's head during the first dinner, before Haman had built gallows for Mordecai and before the king had been reminded of Mordecai's valiant act in saving his life—the king may have become defensive of Haman rather than act in justice. After all, Haman was close to him in many ways. But because Esther stayed tied to the Lord's leading, seeking Him first through communal fasting and prayer, she was able to remain in His providential care and His perfect timing.

The major problem believers face in getting off course from the pathway of purpose God has for them is not God failing to be God. The major problem is we are so misaligned from Him as well as so reactive to the changing situations all around us that we miss seeing Him and what He is doing, especially when negative circumstances come our way. We are ducking and hollering rather than moving gently in alignment toward Him.

The Victory Lap

We've now come to chapter 9 in the book of Esther where we discover that the Jews' freedom to defend themselves led them to so much more than just defense. In fact, they became the ones in charge on the once-intended day of their doom. We read:

> The king's command and law went into effect on the thir-teenth day of the twelfth month, the month Adar. On the day when the Jews' enemies had hoped to overpower them, just the opposite happened. The Jews overpowered those who hated them. In each of King Ahasuerus's provinces the Jews assembled in their cities to attack those who intended to harm them. Not a single person could withstand them; fear of them fell on every nationality. (vv. 1–2)

This happened twelve months after Haman had originally set a plan in motion to destroy the Jews. The narrative makes a point to draw our attention to the fact that "on the day" when Haman had hoped to carry out their destruction, God turned it around so that the "Jews themselves gained mastery over those who hated them" (v. 1 NASB). God turned it around. On the very day the Jews had been selected for defeat by their enemy, God flipped the script entirely. It wasn't a day before. It wasn't even months before. God waited until the very day where they were set to be slaughtered and He turned it to the contrary.

On that day.

Just in case you didn't know it, all of us have a "that day." All of us have a target on our backs put there by the enemy himself (Eph. 6:10–18). Scripture calls it the "evil day" (v. 13). That's the day the devil has determined to do you in. It's the day Satan has determined to destroy your life. It's the day when the enemy wants to bring about the culmination of all the attacks he's put on you and ruin your future with the intersection of it all.

But just as Satan builds his strategy of defeat in your life, God sets up things along the way for victory. Every move the devil makes, you can be assured that God's got two. God is always moving over a period of time to bring about His intended conclusion at the exact right time. Thus, God will even allow the evil to develop and perpetuate itself in order to situate the evil in the right place so that while He is delivering you, He is also destroying it. And in so doing, "that day" becomes a bigger day than the original day when it was planned.

In Esther's case, by the time we get to the day of destruction for the Jews, Haman is already dead. And God is getting ready to wipe out everyone who stood against the Jews in agreement with Haman. God always has a bigger plan than what you can see.

Has God ever released you from something, only to have the problem come back at you? This is similar to the Israelites running from Pharaoh when they first thought they'd been set free, only to have Pharaoh barge in after them because he changed his mind when God hardened his heart. Has God ever set you free from something only to have the very thing you thought had been solved come right back at you again? You thought you would never have to deal with the issue again—you thought you were far from it, or from them. You thought you wouldn't have to deal with that boss anymore. Or those finances. Or that health issue. Only to discover that it looked as if God had done a number on you and what appeared to be a blessing devolved into a curse.

The reason why God will allow these apparent frustrations is because He is after something greater than what you see, and He lines up all of the pieces in order to usher in His swift judgment and deliverance. God will sometimes allow things to get worse because He is after a bigger goal. In other words, He makes things worse to show how big a deliverer He can be. He does it with different strokes for different folks, and His ways are rarely repetitive in nature. But when you cannot trust what you see, you must always trust what you know. He is maneuvering the pathways of life toward His intended kingdom purpose.

Once you understand the assurance of this doctrine of providence and how to remain in alignment with God under His rule, when things do get worse in your life, you will no longer have to react to what you see. Rather, you can rest in the One you know who allowed it to happen. You can rest because you know He is up to something great.

When you cannot trust what you see, you must always trust what you know.

Take Mordecai for example. Not only did Mordecai get delivered from personal doom, but we read in Esther 9:4 that, "For Mordecai exercised great power in the palace, and his fame spread throughout the provinces as he became more and more powerful." Mordecai actually got promoted through the series of events designed to destroy him. The Jews also rose up and not only defended themselves but defeated an enemy who had been bent on their elimination.

Keep in mind, the Jews didn't simply sit back and declare the battle to be won. They rose up and fought their way to victory. Friend, God's providential pathways are not glistening with gold for you to easily skate across. They are often difficult, cobblestone roads requiring your effort and attention with every step. In spiritual warfare, you do not sit on the side and watch God work it all out. Spiritual warfare means you must get involved. You must take up your sword and fight. You must do what Ephesians 6:10–18 calls us to do in putting on the full armor of God as your weapons of warfare. You can't just pray for deliverance and then not go deliverance-hunting. You must apply the spiritual to the situational in order for God's purposes and power to work through your obedience. You must intentionally use whatever legitimate resources God has provided you because God has called you to be involved in the battle.

Exodus 17 gives us a glimpse into the critical need of our involvement. When Israel was fighting their enemies, Moses sat on a rock with his hands held up. Scripture tells us that as long as his hands were held up, Israel prevailed in the battle. But the moment Moses dropped his hands, Israel would start losing the fight. Why did Moses have to hold up his hands while grasping onto the rod of God? Because he had to make heaven the central point of reference for the battle on earth.

There will be things you have to fight through on the pathways to your purpose. There will be problems you have to face. There will be situations you have to negotiate. There will be times you'll need to maneuver as Esther did using her clout with the king. There will be circumstances that call for your action. You cannot possibly just sit by and trust God to do it all. He is the One preparing the pathways, but He calls you to walk on them. Waiting on God's timing and being led by His Spirit does not mean doing nothing. Waiting on God means not going outside of God to do something He didn't call for. Waiting on God means staying tethered to His leading and not disobeying Him in trying to force His hand. Because as long as you are operating within the will of God based on the Word of God, you are situated to see God move providentially in your circumstances.

The point being: You must be moving too.

The Jewish people entered the fight that the king allowed them to take part in. After the first day of battle, the king asked Esther what else she wanted from him. Seeing the open door, Esther asked for another day for the Jews to fight. What's more, she asked for the ten sons of Haman who had been captured to be hanged on the gallows as well. Once again, the king granted Esther her request.

Extending the battle by another day gave the Jews the victory they had been waiting for. During the next day, they killed 75,000 of their enemies. In football, when you want to run the score up on somebody, that means you have already won the game. There is still time left on the clock and the team in the lead continues to score touchdowns just to make a point. When a team is running up the score, they are letting the other team know who is in charge. They are making a big deal out of how bad this loss really is in order to drive home a point. God used Esther to make a point. The point being to get rid of the entirety of what you are facing, not just a part of it.

If you remember from earlier on in this story, the only reason Haman was in the position he held was because King Saul had refused to kill King Agag and all of the Agagites and Amalekites (1 Sam. 15). Saul had disobeyed God in refusing to wipe out an enemy who later came back to haunt the Jews. So this time Esther asked for another day in order to finish what a previous Jewish king wasn't able to. Because Saul had refused to deal with the problem the way God instructed him to many years before, Esther and those under her influence were called upon to deal with it.

Similar issues can arise in our own lives when God instructs us to remove a sin or addictive behavior from our lives, but we only knock out a portion, and not the whole. When you don't cut a sin off completely in your personal life, you leave the door open for that cancer to grow, spread, and take over. Whatever you leave behind can later manifest itself and destroy you. Esther knew this principle and wanted the enemy of the Jews entirely wiped out. She knew that there were generational repercussions for past failures. Generational irresponsibility leads to lifetimes of oppression, addiction, and waste. Esther wanted to solve the problem right then and there, so she sought the king for another day of battle. Her strategic mind was cleverer than the former king of her people, which goes to show you that God is no respecter of persons, nor gender, when it comes to accomplishing His plan and purposes; He positions and empowers the people through whom He will accomplish His will. The queen finished the job that the former king hadn't been able to.

Remember God's Providence

Esther then concluded her battle plan by establishing a celebration. The story ends by letting us know that Esther, along with

Mordecai, put in place an annual celebration called Purim. This celebration was to commemorate the unique deliverance God had provided for the Jews to not only survive an edict of death against them, but to turn it around and secure a full, decisive victory over their enemies. We read:

> Queen Esther, daughter of Abihail, along with Mordecai the Jew, wrote this second letter with full authority to confirm the letter about Purim. He sent letters with assurances of peace and security to all the Jews who were in the 127 provinces of the kingdom of Ahasuerus, in order to confirm these days of Purim at their proper time just as Mordecai the Jew and Esther the queen had established them and just as they had committed themselves and their descendants to the practices of fasting and lamentation. So Esther's command confirmed these customs of Purim, which were then written into the record. (Esther 9:29–32)

The name of this annual remembrance and celebration was taken from the word *Pur*. You'll remember in Esther 3:7, that it was Pur that Haman used to determine the date the Jews would be killed. It says, "In the first month, the month of Nisan, in King Ahasuerus's twelfth year, the Pur—that is, the lot—was cast before Haman for each day in each month, and it fell on the twelfth month, the month Adar." Now, not only did the Jews survive, but Queen Esther created a holiday named *Purim* to celebrate this twist of events that Haman had originally set in motion.

182

See, *Pur* had to do with luck. It had to do with throwing the dice to determine something. So the Jews decided to drive the point home that there is no such thing as luck. The dice didn't determine the date of their destruction. Rather, God providentially determined the date of their victory. And while the days inched closer to what one side thought was certain victory for them, God was arranging the circumstances to bring about victory on the other side.

Esther's celebration—a holiday which is still remembered and honored to this day—was to remind the Jews that God is a providential God. God intervenes on behalf of His people against the evil set to destroy them. He intervenes in order to usher in His kingdom purposes. The story of Esther reminds us that sovereignty is stronger than human strategy, and that providence overrules mankind's plans.

> *The story of Esther reminds us that sovereignty is stronger than human strategy, and that providence overrules mankind's plans.*

God is a God of Purim. He is a God of providence. No matter what others have done to you, they don't determine where the dice fall. I don't care what your finances, health, or circumstances have done to you; they don't determine where things are going to wind up. Only God sets in motion what is final in your life. It is God who makes the intersections on the pathways to your purpose.

Your responsibility is to remain tied to His Word and in close proximity with His Spirit so that each step you take is the one He's guiding you to take. Step by step, you'll get there. Yes, some steps are harder than others. Some hills are steeper than others. Some treks are more treacherous than others. But all are necessary in getting you where God wants you to go. You don't have to see the destination when you set out on your journey. You just have to know the One who can. He'll guide, direct, and sustain you as you just stay close to Him every step along the path.

He knows the way. He knows the play. He's writing the script. He's setting the stage. He's changing the scenes. Casting the characters. You just need to obey His direction in this grand, spectacular story known as your life.

APPENDIX A

Scriptures on Sovereignty

"Yours, Lord, is the greatness and the power and the glory and the splendor and the majesty, for everything in the heavens and on earth belongs to you. Yours, Lord, is the kingdom, and you are exalted as head over all. Riches and honor come from you, and you are the ruler of everything. Power and might are in your hand, and it is in your hand to make great and to give strength to all." (1 Chron. 29:11–12)

Our God is in heaven and does whatever he pleases. (Ps. 115:3)

A person's heart plans his way, but the Lord determines his steps. (Prov. 16:9)

I know that you can do anything and no plan of yours can be thwarted. (Job 42:2)

"Remember what happened long ago, for I am God, and there is no other; I am God, and no one is like me. I declare the end from the beginning, and from long ago what is not yet done, saying: my plan will take place, and I will do all my will." (Isa. 46:9–10)

Many plans are in a person's heart, but the LORD's decree will prevail. (Prov. 19:21)

The LORD has established his throne in heaven, and his kingdom rules over all. (Ps. 103:19)

And we know that God causes all things to work together for good to those who love God, to those who are called according to His purpose. (Rom. 8:28 NASB)

So then, he has mercy on whom he wants to have mercy and he hardens whom he wants to harden. (Rom. 9:18)

All the inhabitants of the earth are counted as nothing, and he does what he wants with the army of heaven and the inhabitants of the earth. There is no one who can block his hand or say to him, "What have you done?" (Dan. 4:35)

The LORD does whatever he pleases in heaven and on earth, in the seas and all the depths. (Ps. 135:6)

In him we have also received an inheritance, because we were predestined according to the plan of the one who works out everything in agreement with the purpose of his will. (Eph. 1:11)

Or has the potter no right over the clay, to make from the same lump one piece of pottery for honor and another for dishonor? (Rom. 9:21)

Who is there who speaks and it happens, unless the LORD has ordained it? (Lam. 3:37)

The LORD has prepared everything for his purpose—even the wicked for the day of disaster. (Prov. 16:4)

In him we have also received an inheritance, because we were pre-destined according to the plan of the one who works out every-thing in agreement with the purpose of his will, so that we who had already put our hope in Christ might bring praise to his glory. (Eph. 1:11–12)

The lot is cast into the lap, but its every decision is from the LORD. (Prov. 16:33)

"I form light and create darkness, I make success and create disas-ter; I am the LORD, who does all these things." (Isa. 45:7)

A king's heart is like channeled water in the LORD's hand: He directs it wherever he chooses. (Prov. 21:1)

You will say to me, therefore, "Why then does he still find fault? For who can resist his will?" But who are you, a mere man, to talk back to God? Will what is formed say to the one who formed it, "Why did you make me like this?" (Rom. 9:19–20)

"No one can come to me unless the Father who sent me draws him, and I will raise him up on the last day." (John 6:44)

God will bring this about in his own time. He is the blessed and only Sovereign, the King of kings, and Lord of lords. (1 Tim. 6:15)

"See now that I alone am he; there is no God but me. I bring death and I give life; I wound and I heal. No one can rescue anyone from my power." (Deut. 32:39)

"Look, I am the Lord, the God over every creature. Is anything too difficult for me?" (Jer. 32:27)

He said: "Lord, God of our ancestors, are you not the God who is in heaven, and do you not rule over all the kingdoms of the nations? Power and might are in your hand, and no one can stand against you." (2 Chron. 20:6)

The Lord of Armies himself has planned it; therefore, and who can stand in its way? It is his hand that is outstretched, so who can turn it back? (Isa. 14:27)

The Lord of Armies has sworn: As I have purposed, so it will be; as I have planned it, so it will happen. (Isa. 14:24)

For he chose us in him, before the foundation of the world, to be holy and blameless in love before him. (Eph. 1:4)

"I declare the end from the beginning, and from long ago that which is not yet done, saying: my plan will take place, and I will do all my will." (Isa. 46:10)

Oh, Lord GOD! You yourself have made the heavens and earth by your great power and with your outstretched arm. Nothing is too difficult for you! (Jer. 32:17)

For we are his workmanship, created in Christ Jesus for good works, which God prepared ahead of time for us to do. (Eph. 2:10)

"You planned evil against me; God planned it for good to bring about the present result—the survival of many people." (Gen. 50:20)

"By my great strength and outstretched arm, I made the earth, and the people, and animals on the face of the earth. I give it to anyone I please." (Jer. 27:5)

"Also from today on I am he alone, and none can rescue from my power. I act, and who can reverse it?" (Isa. 43:13)

For it is God who is working in you both to will and to work according to his good purpose. (Phil. 2:13)

When the Gentiles heard this, they rejoiced and honored the word of the Lord, and all who had been appointed to eternal life believed. (Acts 13:48)

But he is unchangeable; who can oppose him? He does what he desires. (Job 23:13)

Though he was delivered up according to God's determined plan and foreknowledge, you used lawless people to nail him to a cross and kill him. (Acts 2:23)

The LORD brings death and gives life; he sends down to Sheol and raises others up. (1 Sam. 2:6)

For everything was created by him, in heaven and on earth, the visible and the invisible, whether thrones or dominions or rulers or authorities—all things have been created through him and for him. (Col. 1:16)

Wisdom and strength belong to God; counsel and understanding are his. Whatever he tears down cannot be rebuilt; whoever he imprisons cannot be released. (Job 12:13–14)

In the beginning God created the heavens and the earth. (Gen. 1:1)

He changes the times and seasons; he removes kings and establishes kings. He gives wisdom to the wise and knowledge to those who have understanding. (Dan. 2:21)

Consider the work of God, for who can straighten out what he has made crooked? In the day of prosperity be joyful, but in the day of adversity, consider: God has made the one as well as the other, so that no one can discover anything that will come after him. (Eccles. 7:13–14)

No wisdom, no understanding, and no counsel will prevail against the LORD. (Prov. 21:30)

Can any of the worthless idols of the nations bring rain? Or can the skies alone give showers? Are you not the LORD our God? We therefore put our hope in you, for you have done all these things. (Jer. 14:22)

"Wisdom and strength belong to God; counsel and understanding are his. Whatever he tears down cannot be rebuilt; whoever he imprisons cannot be released. When he withholds water, everything dries up, and when he releases it, it destroys the land. True wisdom and power belong to him. The deceived and the deceiver are his." (Job 12:13–16)

For though her sons had not been born yet or done anything good or bad, so that God's purpose according to election might stand—not from works but from the one who calls. (Rom. 9:11–12a)

He makes nations great, then destroys them; he enlarges nations, then leads them away. (Job 12:23)

Jesus looked at them and said, "With man this is impossible, but with God all things are possible." (Matt. 19:26)

How countless are your works, LORD! In wisdom you have made them all; the earth is full of your creatures. (Ps. 104:24)

"Very well," the LORD told Satan, "everything he owns is in your power. However, do not lay a hand on Job himself." So Satan left the LORD's presence. (Job 1:12)

"But remember that the LORD your God gives you the power to gain wealth, in order to confirm his covenant he swore to your fathers, as it is today." (Deut. 8:18)

He is before all things, and by him all things hold together. (Col. 1:17)

The eyes of the LORD are everywhere, observing the wicked and the good. (Prov. 15:3)

Those who oppose the LORD will be shattered; he will thunder in the heavens against them. The LORD will judge the ends of the earth. He will give power to his king; he will lift up the horn of his anointed. (1 Sam. 2:10)

Now to the King eternal, immortal, invisible, the only God, be honor and glory forever and ever. Amen. (1 Tim. 1:17)

For those he foreknew he also predestined to be conformed to the image of his Son, so that he would be the firstborn among many brothers and sisters. (Rom. 8:29)

All things were created through him, and apart from him not one thing was created that has been created. In him was life, and that life was the light of men. (John 1:3–4)

Do not both adversity and good come from the mouth of the Most High? (Lam. 3:38)

I know, LORD, that a person's way of life is not his own; no one who walks determines his own steps. (Jer. 10:23)

No creature is hidden from him, but all things are naked and exposed to the eyes of him to whom we must give an account. (Heb. 4:13)

For from him and through him and to him are all things. To him be the glory forever. Amen. (Rom. 11:36)

He said, "This is why I told you that no one can come to me unless it is granted to him by the Father." (John 6:65)

The LORD sits enthroned over the flood; the LORD sits enthroned, King forever. (Ps. 29:10)

"Very well," the LORD told Satan, "he is in your power; only spare his life." (Job 2:6)

The LORD said to him, "Who placed a mouth on humans? Who makes a person mute or deaf, seeing or blind? Is it not I, the LORD?" (Exod. 4:11)

"For my thoughts are not your thoughts, and your ways are not my ways." This is the LORD's declaration. "For as heaven is higher than earth, so my ways are higher than your ways, and my thoughts than your thoughts. For just as rain and snow fall from heaven and do not return there without saturating the earth and making it germinate and sprout, and providing seed to sow and food to eat, so my word that comes from my mouth will not return to me empty, but it will accomplish what I please and will prosper in what I send it to do." (Isa. 55:8–11)

Your eyes saw me when I was formless; all my days were written in your book and planned before a single one of them began. (Ps. 139:16)

"The heavens, indeed the highest heavens, belong to the Lord your God, as does the earth and everything in it." (Deut. 10:14)

Paul, a servant of God and an apostle of Jesus Christ, for the faith of God's elect and their knowledge of the truth that leads to godliness. (Titus 1:1)

I am sure of this, that he who started a good work in you will carry it on to completion until the day of Christ Jesus. (Phil. 1:6)

If a ram's horn is blown in a city, aren't people afraid? If a disaster occurs in a city, hasn't the Lord done it? (Amos 3:6)

God is enthroned above the circle of the earth; its inhabitants are like grasshoppers. He stretches out the heavens like thin cloth and spreads them out like a tent to live in. (Isa. 40:22)

"You speak as a foolish woman speaks," he told her. "Should we accept only good from God and not adversity?" Throughout all this Job did not sin in what he said. (Job 2:10)

All who live on the earth will worship it, everyone whose name was not written from the foundation of the world in the book of life of the Lamb who was slaughtered. (Rev. 13:8)

"Everyone the Father gives me will come to me, and the one who comes to me I will never cast out." (John 6:37)

In the beginning was the Word, and the Word was with God, and the Word was God. He was with God in the beginning. All things were created through him, and apart from him not one thing was created that has been created. In him was life, and that life was the light of men. That light shines in the darkness, and yet the darkness did not overcome it. (John 1:1–5)

Jesus came near and said to them, "All authority has been given to me in heaven and on earth." (Matt. 28:18)

God had granted Daniel kindness and compassion from the chief eunuch. (Dan. 1:9)

A horse is prepared for the day of battle, but victory comes from the LORD. (Prov. 21:31)

They observed the Festival of Unleavened Bread for seven days with joy, because the LORD had made them joyful, having changed the Assyrian king's attitude toward them, so that he supported them in the work on the house of the God of Israel. (Ezra 6:22)

But Joseph said to them, "Don't be afraid. Am I in the place of God? You planned evil against me; God planned it for good to bring about the present result—the survival of many people. Therefore don't be afraid. I will take care of you and your children." And he comforted them and spoke kindly to them. (Gen. 50:19–21)

But we do see Jesus—made lower than the angels for a short time so that by God's grace he might taste death for everyone—crowned with glory and honor because he suffered death. (Heb. 2:9)

For whatever was written in the past was written for our instruction, so that we may have hope through endurance and through the encouragement from the Scriptures. (Rom. 15:4)

For those he foreknew he also predestined to be conformed to the image of his Son, so that he would be the firstborn among many brothers and sisters. And those he predestined, he also called; and those he called, he also justified; and those he justified, he also glorified. (Rom. 8:29–30)

As soon as it was night, the brothers and sisters sent Paul and Silas away to Berea. Upon arrival, they went into the synagogue of the Jews. The people here were of more noble character than those in Thessalonica, since they received the word with eagerness and examined the Scriptures daily to see if these things were so. (Acts 17:10–11)

Acknowledge that the LORD is God. He made us, and we are his— his people and the sheep of his pasture. (Ps. 100:3)

Can you fasten the chains of the Pleiades or loosen the belt of Orion? Can you bring out the constellations in their season and lead the Bear and her cubs? Do you know the laws of heaven? Can you impose its authority on earth? (Job 38:31–33)

And he said, "The LORD has sworn; the LORD will have war against Amalek from generation to generation." (Exod. 17:16 NASB)

Keeping our eyes on Jesus, the source and perfecter of faith. For the joy that lay before him, he endured the cross, despising the shame, and sat down at the right hand of the throne of God. (Heb. 12:2)

For it has been granted to you on Christ's behalf not only to believe in him, but also to suffer for him. (Phil. 1:29)

For you are saved by grace through faith, and this is not from yourselves; it is God's gift—not from works, so that no one can boast. (Eph. 2:8–9)

"I am the vine; you are the branches. The one who remains in me and I in him produces much fruit, because you can do nothing without me." (John 15:5)

"For God loved the world in this way: He gave his one and only Son, so that everyone who believes in him will not perish but have eternal life. For God did not send his Son into the world to condemn the world, but to save the world through him." (John 3:16–17)

He is the image of the invisible God, the firstborn over all creation. For everything was created by him, in heaven and on earth, the visible and invisible, whether thrones or dominions or rulers or authorities—all things have been created through him and for him. (Col. 1:15–16)

"You would have no authority over me at all," Jesus answered him, "if it hadn't been given you from above. This is why the one who handed me over to you has the greater sin." (John 19:11)

APPENDIX B

The Urban Alternative

The Urban Alternative (TUA) equips, empowers, and unites Christians to impact *individuals*, *families*, *churches*, and *communities* through a thoroughly kingdom agenda worldview. In teaching truth, we seek to transform lives.

The core cause of the problems we face in our personal lives, homes, churches, and societies is a spiritual one; therefore, the only way to address it is spiritually. We've tried a political, social, economic, and even a religious agenda.

It's time for a **kingdom agenda**.

The kingdom agenda can be defined as the visible manifestation of the comprehensive rule of God over every area of life.

The unifying central theme throughout the Bible is the glory of God and the advancement of His kingdom. The conjoining thread from Genesis to Revelation—from beginning to end—is focused on one thing: God's glory through advancing God's kingdom.

When you do not have that theme, the Bible becomes disconnected stories that are great for inspiration but seem to be unrelated in purpose and direction. The Bible exists to share God's movement in history toward the establishment and expansion of His kingdom highlighting the connectivity throughout which is the kingdom. Understanding that increases the relevancy of this several thousand-year-old manuscript to your day-to-day living, because the kingdom is not only then, it is now.

The absence of the kingdom's influence in our personal and family lives, churches and communities has led to a deterioration in our world of immense proportions:

- People live segmented, compartmentalized lives because they lack God's kingdom worldview.
- Families disintegrate because they exist for their own satisfaction rather than for the kingdom.
- Churches are limited in the scope of their impact because they fail to comprehend that the goal of the church is not the church itself but the kingdom.
- Communities have nowhere to turn to find real solutions for real people who have real problems because the church has become divided, in-grown, and unable to transform the cultural landscape in any relevant way.

The kingdom agenda offers us a way to see and live life with a solid hope by optimizing the solutions of heaven. When God, and His rule, is no longer the final and authoritative standard under which all else falls, order and hope leaves with Him. But the reverse of that is true as well: As long as you have God, you have hope. If God is still in the picture, and as long as His agenda is still on the table, it's not over.

Even if relationships collapse, God will sustain you. Even if finances dwindle, God will keep you. Even if dreams die, God will revive you. As long as God, and His rule, is still the overarching rule in your life, family, church, and community, there is always hope.

Our world needs the King's agenda. Our churches need the King's agenda. Our families need the King's agenda.

In many major cities, there is a loop that drivers can take when they want to get somewhere on the other side of the city, but don't necessarily want to head straight through downtown. This loop will take you close enough to the city so that you can see its towering buildings and skyline, but not close enough to actually experience it.

This is precisely what we, as a culture, have done with God. We have put Him on the "loop" of our personal, family, church, and community lives. He's close enough to be at hand should we need Him in an emergency, but far enough away that He can't be the center of who we are.

We want God on the "loop," not the King of the Bible who comes downtown into the very heart of our ways. Leaving God on the "loop" brings about dire consequences as we have seen in our own lives and with others. But when we make God, and His rule, the centerpiece of all we think, do, or say, it is then that we will experience Him in the way He longs to be experienced by us.

He wants us to be kingdom people with kingdom minds set on fulfilling His kingdom's purposes. He wants us to pray, as Jesus did, "Not my will, but Thy will be done." Because His is the kingdom, the power, and the glory.

There is only one God, and we are not Him. As King and Creator, God calls the shots. It is only when we align ourselves underneath His comprehensive hand that we will access His full power and authority in all spheres of life: personal, familial, church, and community.

As we learn how to govern ourselves under God, we then transform the institutions of family, church, and society from a biblically based kingdom worldview.

Under Him, we touch heaven and change Earth.

To achieve our goal we use a variety of strategies, approaches, and resources for reaching and equipping as many people as possible.

Broadcast Media

Millions of individuals experience *The Alternative with Dr. Tony Evans* through the daily radio broadcast playing on nearly **fourteen**

hundred RADIO outlets and in more than **one hundred and thirty countries**. The broadcast can also be seen on several television networks, and is viewable online at TonyEvans.org. You can also listen or view the daily broadcast by downloading the Tony Evans app for free in the App store. More than **ten million** message downloads occur each year.

Leadership Training

The Tony Evans Training Center (TETC) facilitates educational programming that embodies the ministry philosophy of Dr. Tony Evans as expressed through the kingdom agenda. The training courses focus on leadership development and discipleship in the following five tracks:

- Bible and Theology
- Personal Growth
- Family and Relationships
- Church Health and Leadership Development
- Society and Community Impact Strategies

The TETC program includes courses for both local and online students. Furthermore, TETC programming includes course work for nonstudent attendees. Pastors, Christian leaders, and Christian laity, both local and at a distance, can seek out The Kingdom Agenda Certificate for personal, spiritual, and professional development. Some courses are valued for CEU credit as well as viable in transferring for college credit with our partner school(s). For more information, visit: tonyevanstraining.org.

The Kingdom Agenda Pastors (KAP) provides a *viable network for like-minded pastors* who embrace the Kingdom Agenda philosophy. Pastors have the opportunity to go deeper with Dr. Tony Evans as they are given greater biblical knowledge, practical applications, and resources to impact individuals, families, churches, and communities. KAP welcomes *senior and associate pastors* of all churches. KAP also offers an annual Summit held each year in Dallas with intensive seminars, workshops, and resources.

Pastors' Wives Ministry, founded by Dr. Lois Evans, provides *counsel, encouragement, and spiritual resources* for pastors' wives as they serve with their husbands in the ministry. A primary focus of the ministry is the KAP Summit that offers senior pastors' wives a safe place to *reflect, renew,* and *relax* along with training in personal development, spiritual growth, and care for their emotional and physical well-being.

Community Impact

National Church Adopt-A-School Initiative (NCAASI) prepares churches across the country to impact communities by using *public schools as the primary vehicle for effecting positive social change* in urban youth and families. Leaders of churches, school districts, faith-based organizations, and other nonprofit organizations are equipped with the knowledge and tools to *forge partnerships* and build *strong social service delivery systems*. This training is based on the comprehensive church-based community impact strategy conducted by Oak Cliff Bible Fellowship. It addresses such areas as economic development, education, housing, health revitalization, family renewal, and racial reconciliation. We assist churches in tailoring the model to meet specific needs of their communities while simultaneously addressing the spiritual and moral frame of reference. Training events are held annually in the Dallas area at Oak Cliff Bible Fellowship.

Athlete's Impact (AI) exists as an outreach both into and through the sports arena. Coaches are the most influential factor in young people's lives, even ahead of their parents. With the growing rise of fatherlessness in our culture, more young people are looking to their coaches for guidance, character development, practical needs, and hope. After Coaches on the influencer scale fall athletes. Athletes (whether professional or amateur) influence younger athletes and kids within their spheres of impact. Knowing this, we have made it our aim to equip and train Coaches and athletes on how to live out and utilize their God-given roles for the benefit of the kingdom. We aim to do this through our iCoach App, weCoach Football Conference, as well as resources such as *The Playbook: A Life Strategy Guide for Athletes*.

Resource Development

We are fostering lifelong learning partnerships with the people we serve by providing a variety of published materials. Dr. Evans has published more than one hundred unique titles based on over forty years of preaching whether that is in booklet, book, or Bible study format. The goal is to strengthen individuals in their walk with God and service to others.

For more information, and a complimentary copy of Dr. Evans' devotional newsletter, call (800) 800-3222 *or* write TUA at P. O. Box 4000, Dallas, TX, 75208, *or* visit us online at www.TonyEvans.org.

NOTES

1. https://www.newsday.com/sports/columnists/bob-glauber/super-bowl
-lii-doug-pederson-eagles-1.16503211, by Bob Glauber, "Eagles Coach
Doug Pederson Had a Rough Start in Philadelphia," February 3, 2018,
accessed February 8, 2018.

2. https://www.espn.com/nfl/story/_/id/22326016/nick-foles-philadelphia
-eagles-named-mvp-super-bowl-lii

3. https://www.si.com/nfl/2018/02/07/super-bowl-52-film-study-notes
-new-england-patriots-philadelphia-eagles

4. https://sports.good.is/articles/wentz-foles-message

Tony EVANS
THE URBAN ALTERNATIVE

YOUR *Eternity* IS OUR *Priority*

At The Urban Alternative, eternity is our priority—for the individual, the family, the church and the nation. The 45-year teaching ministry of Tony Evans has allowed us to reach a world in need with:

The Alternative – Our flagship radio program brings hope and comfort to an audience of millions on over 1,400 radio outlets across the country.

tonyevans.org – Our library of teaching resources provides solid Bible teaching through the inspirational books and sermons of Tony Evans.

Tony Evans Training Center – Experience the adventure of God's Word with our online classroom, providing at-your-own-pace courses for your PC or mobile device.

Tony Evans app – Packed with audio and video clips, devotionals, Scripture readings and dozens of other tools, the mobile app provides inspiration on-the-go.

Explore God's kingdom today.
Live for more than the moment.
Live for *eternity.*

tonyevans.org

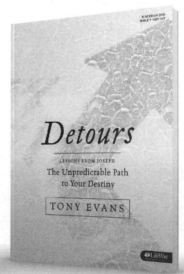